LETTERS OF NOTE: NEW YORK CITY

Letters of Note was born in 2009 with the launch
of lettersofnote.com, a website celebrating
old-fashioned correspondence that has since
been visited over 100 million times. The first
Letters of Note volume was published in October
2013, followed later that year by the first
Letters Live, an event at which world-class
performers delivered remarkable letters
to a live audience.

Since then, these two siblings have grown side
by side, with *Letters of Note* becoming an
international phenomenon, and Letters
Live shows being staged at iconic venues
around the world, from London's Royal Albert Hall
to the theatre at the Ace Hotel in Los Angeles.

You can find out more at lettersofnote.com and
letterslive.com. And now you can also listen to the
audio editions of the new series of *Letters of Note*,
read by an extraordinary cast drawn from the
wealth of talent that regularly takes part in
the acclaimed Letters Live shows.

Letters of Note

NEW YORK CITY

COMPILED BY

Shaun Usher

PENGUIN BOOKS

For all New Yorkers

PENGUIN BOOKS
An imprint of Penguin Random House LLC
penguinrandomhouse.com

First published in Great Britain as *Letters of Note: New York* by
Canongate Books Ltd 2021
Published in Penguin Books 2021

LIBRARY OF CONGRESS CATALOGING-IN-PUBLICATION DATA
Names: Usher, Shaun, 1978– compiler.
Title: Letters of note : New York City / compiled by Shaun Usher.
Description: [New York, New York] : Penguin Books, 2021. |
Series: Letters of note |
Identifiers: LCCN 2021027956 (print) | LCCN 2021027957 (ebook) |
ISBN 9780143134688 (paperback) | ISBN 9780525506492 (ebook)
Subjects: LCSH: Letters. | New York (N.Y.)—History—Sources. |
New York (N.Y.)—Social life and customs—Sources.
Classification: LCC F128 .L48 2021 (print) |
LCC F128 (ebook) | DDC 974.7/1—dc23
LC record available at https://lccn.loc.gov/2021027956
LC ebook record available at https://lccn.loc.gov/2021027957

Printed in the United States of America
1st Printing

Set in Joanna MT

CONTENTS

A letter is a time bomb, a message in a bottle,
a spell, a cry for help, a story, an expression of
concern, a ladle of love, a way to connect through
words. This simple and brilliantly democratic art
form remains a potent means of communication
and, regardless of whatever technological revolution
we are in the middle of, the letter lives and, like
literature, it always will.

INTRODUCTION

Welcome to *Letters of Note: New York*, a love letter to a city which, despite almost defying description, has thankfully been described countless times in correspondence. It features in the letters of those who have lived in it, the correspondence of those who have been drawn to it, the correspondence of those who have fallen in love with it from afar, the correspondence of those who have rolled up their sleeves to help build it, and, of course, the correspondence of those to whom such an immense concentration of human energy, concrete and curious smells is entirely unappealing.

To cover every aspect of a city so diverse and thrillingly alive would be an impossibility in a book ten times the length of the pocket-sized anthology you now hold. However, in these pages you will find a taste of all of the above, including a dazzling description of the view from atop the Empire State Building, written by a lady without the benefit of sight; a successful plea from a former First Lady to save the sparkling jewel that is Grand Central Terminal; and a civil rights giant's letter of complaint to a New York bus company which failed to get him back to Harlem. You'll also read an exhausted letter from a dizzied, hungover Welsh poet who had just arrived on the scene, an exhilarated letter home from an aspiring playwright whose love affair with Broadway was soon to reach awesome heights and a hugely important missive which eventually brought acres of greenery and much-needed fresh air to Manhattan. And then there is the moving letter from the widow of a police officer who, one fateful day in 2001, ran towards the very danger thousands were attempting to flee, and much, much more.

I can vividly remember my first trip to New York City. It was 2002. As the taxicab from JFK Airport slowly slipped out of the Midtown Tunnel and casually joined the streets of the Manhattan I had so often imagined, I was instantly euphoric. Within seconds, I could almost hear my eyeballs screeching in awe. Within minutes, I was physically drunk with excitement. And within hours I had concluded that New York City is impossible. Quite clearly, I told myself, its dimensions make no sense. I am certainly no engineer, I thought, but I am fairly sure those crystalline, razor-thin skyscrapers are too tall, too numerous, too densely situated and too heavy to simply just stand there, unaided. The only answer, I concluded, is that the centre of New York

City has been ripped from a cartoon, or a movie set, or an M. C. Escher lithograph, and brought to life using technology far beyond my comprehension. Some kind of projector, I imagined.

Letters of Note: New York is an homage not just to this magnificent city's five boroughs, but to the people who built it, live in it and take care of it. And may this book also serve as a thank you to the letter writers who have somehow managed to capture, by mail, a snapshot of a city so difficult to adequately describe.

Shaun Usher
2020

The Letters

LETTER 01
I'M IN LOVE WITH N.Y.

Anaïs Nin to Henry Miller

3 December 1934

Born to Cuban parents in the Parisian suburb of Neuilly-sur-Seine, celebrated diarist Anaïs Nin spent her early years moving around Europe and was eleven years old when she, her younger brothers and mother left Barcelona and set sail for New York City, Nin's father having abandoned the family. It was on this long journey that she began to write her now-famous diaries. Nin went on to study and work in New York until 1924, at which point she returned to Paris with her new husband, Hugh Guiler. It would be another ten years until Nin saw New York again, this time in the company of noted psychoanalyst Dr Otto Rank, her therapist and lover. Soon after returning to the city, she wrote a letter to another man with whom she was romantically linked, who was still in Paris: Henry Miller.

THE LETTER

Barbizon Plaza Hotel
6th Ave. & 58th St.
Dec 3, 1934

Henry:

I rushed you a note the other day and have not been able to write a line for myself since. Have let things take their course and since making money for the rent was the first item on the list I accepted the enormous amount of work required by the [Psychological] Center. Next weekend I see about the dancing.

Meanwhile, I'm busy all day, like a big business woman, and then every night somebody says: "Let us show you New York." Americans are like Spaniards. So I have seen shows, Broadway, lunch on top of the Empire State, a dance hall in Harlem, movies at Radio City. I'm in love with N.Y. It matches my mood. I'm not overwhelmed. It is the suitable scene for my ever ever heightened life. I love the proportions, the amplitude, the brilliance, the polish, the solidity. I look up at Radio City insolently and love it. It is all great, and Babylonian. Broadway at night. Cellophane. The newness. The vitality. True, it is only physical. But it's inspiring. Just bring your own contents, and you create a sparkle of the highest power. I'm not moved, not speechless. I stand straight, tough, and I meet the impact. I feel the glow and the dancing in everything. The radio music in the taxis, scientific magic, which can all be used lyrically. That's my last word. Give New York to a poet. He can use it. It can be poetized. Or maybe that's a mania of mine, to poetize. I live lightly, smoothly, actively, ears and eyes wide open, alert, oiled! I feel a kind of exhilaration and the tempo is like that of my blood. I'm at once beyond, over and in New York, tasting it fully.

I don't know if I am telling you enough. I write you between telephone calls, visitors, letters etc. I don't hear myself writing. The only missing element is time. It is rare! We are flying. One goes for the weekend to Washington. One flies to Chicago in four hours. Rank has to go for lectures all over, and leaves me in charge . . .

Write me at the Barbizon. They never send up the mail. I call for it. It is quite safe.

A.

'I LOVE THE
PROPORTIONS, THE
AMPLITUDE, THE
BRILLIANCE, THE
POLISH, THE SOLIDITY.'

— *Anaïs Nin*

LETTER 02
THE BLESSINGS OF PURE AIR
Ambrose Kingsland to Common Council of NYC
5 April 1851

Ambrose Kingsland was sixteen years old when he and his brother founded the successful sperm oil business that would cement the family's already considerable fortune. Arguably, however, his greatest achievement was this letter written decades later in 1851. The population of New York City was expanding at an incredible rate, and as Kingsland approached middle age he yearned to direct his energy and experience towards the fast-evolving city he loved. And so, Ambrose Kingsland ran for mayor, winning by a margin of close to 4,000 votes. One of his first acts as the 71st Mayor of New York was to write to the city's council to recommend that they locate and purchase land on which could be built a public park 'on a scale which will be worthy of the city'. The council agreed; the wheels were set in motion. Eight years later, in the winter of 1859, Central Park – designed by Frederick Law Olmsted and Calvert Vaux – opened to the public.

THE LETTER

TO THE HONORABLE, THE COMMON COUNCIL:

Gentlemen: —
The rapid augmentation of our population, and the
great increase in the value of property in the lower
part of the city, justify me in calling the attention
of your Honorable Body, to the necessity of making
some suitable provision for the wants of our citizens, who are thronging into the upper wards,
which but a few years since were considered as
entirely out of the city. It seems obvious to me that
the entire tongue of land south of the line drawn
across the [City Hall] Park, is destined to be
devoted, entirely and solely, to commercial
purposes; and the Park and Battery, which were
formerly favorite places of resort for pleasure and
recreation, for citizens, whose residences were
below that line, are now deserted. The tide of
population is rapidly flowing to the northern
section of the island, and it is here that provision
should be made for the thousands whose dwellings
will, ere long, fill up the vacant streets and avenues
north of Union Park.

The public places of New York are not in

keeping with the character of our city; nor do they in any wise subserve the purpose for which such places should be set apart. Each year will witness a certain increase in the value of real estate, out of the city proper, and I do not know that any period will be more suitable than the present one, for the purchase and laying out of a park, on a scale which will be worthy of the city.

There are places on the island easily accessible, and possessing all the advantages of wood, lawn and water, which might, at a comparatively small expense, be converted into a park, which would be at once the pride and ornament of the city. Such a park, well laid out, would become the favorite resort of all classes. There are thousands who pass the day of rest among the idle and dissolute, in porter-houses, or in places more objectionable, who would rejoice in being enabled to breathe the pure air in such a place, while the ride and drive through its avenues, free from the noise, dust and confusion inseparable from all thoroughfares, would hold out strong inducements for the affluent to make it a place of resort.

There is no park on the island deserving the name, and while I cannot believe that any one can be found to advance an objection against the expediency of having such a one in our midst,

I think that the expenditure of a sum necessary to procure and lay out a park of sufficient magnitude to answer the purposes above noted, would be well and wisely appropriated, and would be returned to us four fold, in the health, happiness and comfort of those whose interest[s] are specially intrusted to our keeping — the poorer classes.

The establishment of such a park would prove a lasting monument to the wisdom, sagacity and forethought of its founders, and would secure the gratitude of thousands yet unborn, for the blessings of pure air, and the opportunity for innocent, healthful enjoyment.

I commend this subject to your consideration, in the conviction that its importance will insure your careful attention and prompt action.

A. C. KINGSLAND, MAYOR.

Edmund White to Ann and Alfred Corn
July 1969

*On the evening of 27 June 1969, New York City police
raided the Stonewall Inn. The inn was a popular
Mafia-run gay bar in Greenwich Village, frequented by
much of the city's queer community at a time when all
but one US state – Illinois – still deemed homosexual
acts to be illegal. This was the sixth raid in three
weeks. This time, however, the establishment's patrons,
and those of surrounding premises, chose to fight back,
setting in motion protests which led to the gay liberation movement. On the riots' anniversary a year later,
the first Pride march – the Christopher Street
Liberation Day March – began at the inn. In the days
following those riots, novelist Edmund White wrote to
his friends, Ann and Alfred Corn, and described the
events.*

THE LETTER

Dear Ann and Alfred,

Well, the big news here is Gay Power. It's the most extraordinary thing. It all began two weeks ago on a Friday night. The cops raided the Stonewall Inn, that mighty Bastille which you know has remained impregnable for three years, so brazen and so conspicuous that one could only surmise that the Mafia was paying off the pigs handsomely. Apparently, however, a new public official, Sergeant Smith, has taken over the Village, and he's a peculiarly diligent lawman. In any event, a mammoth paddy wagon, as big as a school bus, pulled up to the Wall and about ten cops raided the joint. The kids were all shooed into the street; soon other gay kids and straight spectators swelled the ranks to, I'd say, about a thousand people. Christopher Street was completely blocked off and the crowds swarmed from the Voice office down to the Civil War hospital.

As the Mafia owners were dragged out one by one and shoved into the wagon, the crowd would let out Bronx cheers and jeers and clapping. Someone shouted "Gay Power," others took up the cry--and then it dissolved into giggles. A few more gay prisoners--bartenders, hatcheck boys--a few more cheers, someone starts singing "We Shall Overcome"--and then they started camping on it. A drag queen is shoved into the wagon; she hits the cop over the head with her purse. The cop clubs her. Angry stirring in the crowd. The cops, used to the cringing and disorganization of the gay crowds, snort off. But the crowd doesn't disperse. Everyone is restless, angry and high-spirited. No one has a slogan, no one even has an attitude, but something's brewing.

Some adorable butch hustler boy pulls up a parking meter, mind you, out of the pavement, and uses it as a battering ram (a few cops are still inside the Wall, locked in). The boys begin to pound at the heavy wooden double doors and windows; glass shatters all over the street. Cries of "Liberate the Bar." Bottles (from hostile straights?) rain down from the apartment windows. Cries of "We're the Pink Panthers." A mad Negro queen whirls like a dervish with a twisted piece of metal in her hand and breaks the remaining windows. The door begins to give. The cop turns a hose on the crowd (they're still within the Wall). But they can't aim it properly, and the crowd sticks. Finally the door is broken down and the kids, as though working to a prior plan, systematically dump refuse from the waste cans into the Wall, squirting it with lighter fluid, and ignite it. Huge flashes of flame and billows of smoke.

Now the cops in the paddy wagon return, and two fire engines pull up. Clubs fly. The crowd retreats.

Saturday night, the pink panthers are back full force. The cops form a flying wedge at the Greenwich Avenue end of Christopher and drive the kids down towards Sheridan Square. The panthers, however, run down Waverly, up Gay Street, and come out <u>behind</u> the cops, kicking in a chorus line, taunting, screaming. Dreary middle-class East Side queens stand around disapproving but fascinated, unable to go home, as though torn between their class loyalties, their desire to be respectable, and their longing for freedom. Sheridan Square is cordoned off by the cops. The United Cigar store closes, Riker's closes, the deli closes. No one can pass through the square; to walk up Seventh Avenue, you must detour all the way to Bleeker.

A mad left-wing group of straight kids called the Crazies is trying to organize gay kids, point out that Lindsay is to blame (the Crazies want us to vote for Procaccino, or "Prosciutto," as we call him). A Crazy girl launches into a tirade against Governor Rockefeller, "Whose Empire," she cries,

"Must Be Destroyed." Straight Negro boys put their arms around me and say we're comrades (it's okay with me--in fact, great, the first camaraderie I've felt with blacks in years). Mattachine (our NAACP) hands out leaflets about "what to do if arrested." Some man from the Oscar Wilde bookstore hands out a leaflet describing to newcomers what's going on. I give a stump speech about the need to radicalize, how we must recognize we're part of a vast rebellion of all the repressed. Some jeers, some cheers. Charles Burch plans to make a plastique to hurl at cops.

Sunday night, the Stonewall, now reopened-- though one room is charred and blasted, all lights are smashed, and only a few dim bulbs are burning, no bad liquor being sold--the management posts an announcement: "We appreciate all of you and your efforts to help, but the Stonewall believes in peace. Please end the riots. We believe in peace." Some kids, nonetheless, try to turn over a cop car. Twelve are arrested. Some straight toughs rough up some queens. The queens beat them up. Sheridan Square is again blocked off by the pigs. That same night a group of about seventy-five vigilantes in Queens chops down a wooded part of a park as vengeance against the perverts who are cruising in bushes. "They're endangering our women and children." The Times, which has scarcely mentioned the Sheridan Square riots (a half column, very tame) is now so aroused by the conservation issue that it blasts the "vigs" for their malice toward nature.

Wednesday. The Voice runs two front-page stories on the riots, both snide, both devoted primarily to assuring readers that the authors are straight.

This last weekend, nothing much happened because it was the Fourth of July and everyone was away. Charles Burch has decided it's all a drag. When he hears that gay kids are picketing Independence Hall in Philly because they're being denied their constitutional rights, he says: "But of course, the Founding Fathers didn't intend to protect perverts and criminals." Who knows what will happen this weekend, or this week? I'll keep you posted.

Otherwise, nothing much. I've been going out with a mad boy who tried to kill me last Friday. He's very cute, and I'm sure it'd be a kick, but I think I'll take a rain check on the death scene.

Finished the first act of my play and outlined the second. My sister has a new boyfriend who's got $30 million, two doctorates, working on a third. She met him in the bughouse (shows the advantages of sending your daughter to the best bughouse in town). I'm going out to Chicago in two weeks to help her move.

I miss you both frightfully. No more fun dinners, no endless telephone conversations, no sharing of exquisite sensations, gad, it's awful.

Love, Ed

'EVERYONE IS RESTLESS,
ANGRY AND HIGH-
SPIRITED. NO ONE HAS
A SLOGAN, NO ONE
EVEN HAS AN ATTITUDE,
BUT SOMETHING'S
BREWING.'

— Edmund White

LETTER 04
SHADOWS RUN AFTER ME
Kahlil Gibran to Mary Haskell
1 May 1911

Kahlil Gibran was twelve years old when he first arrived in the US, his mother having emigrated with her four children from their home in the Lebanese village of Bsharri. From a young age, Gibran displayed an artistic flair, and his artwork was exhibited for the first time in Boston in 1904. There, Gibran met Mary Haskell, a private-school headmistress whose immediate and unflinching belief, as well as her ensuing patronage, enabled him to develop his talents without financial pressures. New York City eventually beckoned, and from 1911, when this letter to Gaskell was written, until his death twenty years later, Gibran lived in a studio at 51 West 10th Street where he created art and wrote The Prophet, *a collection of poetry which to this day remains one of the best-selling and most translated books in the history of literature.*

THE LETTER

I run through the streets of this gigantic city, and
shadows run after me. I gaze with a thousand eyes
and listen with a thousand ears all through the day;
and when I come home late at night I find more
things to gaze at and more voices to listen to. New
York is not the place where one finds rest. But did
I come here for rest? I am so glad to be able to
run. I spent yesterday afternoon in the Museum —
and I am astonished to find so many wonderful
things in it. It is surely one of the great museums
in the world in spite of its being only fifty years
old. America is far greater than what people think;
her Destiny is strong and healthy and eager. Just
think, Mary, that fifty years ago there was not a
masterpiece in any of the museums of America.
And now they are seen even in private houses.
Something besides wealth brings the beautiful and
noble things from the old world. It is the Hunger
of the *unwealthy* for public properties. I am so glad
that you are reading *Zarathustra*. I want so much to
read it with you in English. Nietzsche to me is a

sober Dionysus — a superman who lives in forests and fields — a mighty being who loves music and dancing and all joy . . .

O, Mary, why did you send more money? I have enough. You gave me more than enough before I came. May the Heavens bless your open hands. Good night, beloved Mary. I wish you were here now.

Kahlil

'NEW YORK IS NOT THE PLACE WHERE ONE FINDS REST. BUT DID I COME HERE FOR REST?'

— *Kahlil Gibran*

LETTER 05
THEY ARE BEING HAD

E.B. White to Harold Ross

January 1950

When he wasn't writing the award-winning children's books and essays for which he is now celebrated – not least his 1949 love letter to the Big Apple, 'Here Is New York' – E.B. White could often be found ruminating on a subject which invigorated him for many years: the design of New York taxicabs. He deemed these vehicles to be fundamentally flawed – one had mounted a kerb in 1931 and killed his beloved dog, Daisy. His friend Harold Ross, also editor of the New Yorker *magazine, was keenly aware of White's obsession, and would send him any relevant literature that crossed his desk. This letter to Ross, with illustrations, was in response to such an article.*

THE LETTER

Mr. Ross:
I've read this, and thanks.

The controversy is muddied up by a lot of irrelevant factors, plus politics. The thing that would benefit New York, or any other city, would be a cab that is properly designed to fulfill the special function it has to perform. These cabs are not so designed. They are simply slight modifications of pleasure cars—and a pleasure car is about the poorest object you could get, as a model. Taxicabs are long and low because for thirty years automobile manufacturers have been boasting of long, low cars. I have personally measured the opening (vertical distance) of a cab door. It is roughly 38 inches. A taxicab is the only thing I know of that expects its patron to enter and leave by an opening 38 inches high. If you had to enter your apartment, your subway, your saloon, your bank vault, or your hall closet through a 38 inch opening, you would be infuriated, and would rebel. Thirty-eight inches is about one-half the height of a man. It makes sense as the entrance to an igloo because of the temperature factor involved; and it makes sense as the entrance to a small cabin cruiser because a high superstructure has disadvantages at sea. A high roof to a New York taxicab has no disadvantage, it has every advantage. New York cabs should be approximately 16 inches higher, should have a hood approximately 12 inches shorter (slightly smaller motor), and should get shed of all the crap they have inherited in the way of flowing fenders.

Did you know that I had been asked to speak on this subject, and allied subjects, at a symposium on automobile design at the Museum of Modern Art? It is beginning to dawn on people that they are being had.

P.S. I'm not going to speak.

Yrs,

E.B. White

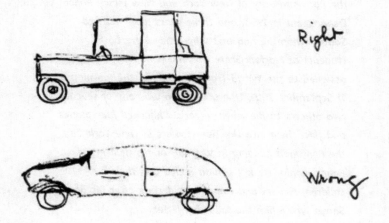

Right

Wrong

LETTER 06
YOU WOULD BE SO PROUD

Sonya Houston to Uhuru Gonja Houston

2011

Uhuru Houston was born in Brooklyn in 1969. He joined the Port Authority of New York and New Jersey Police Department in 1993, and three years later married Sonya, whom he had met when they were both students at Norfolk State University. In 1999, he was assigned to the World Trade Center. On the morning of 11 September 2001, Uhuru Houston was one of seventy-two officers to die when terrorists hijacked four planes and flew them into the Twin Towers in New York City, the Pentagon building in Virginia, and a field in Pennsylvania. He left behind Sonya and their two children, Hasani and Hannah. A decade after his death, Sonya wrote him the following letter.

THE LETTER

Dear Bee,

Yet another gorgeous early fall day, with the temps in the high 70s to low 80s, warm, only a few fluffy cumulus clouds in the sky. The perfect day to be outside . . .

Ten years earlier, the weather was the same. The day our lives would change forever.

By now, we all know the events of that horrific day that would change America and my life forever. No need to go all the way back right now.

I want to fast-forward you to the page we are on now. The book that is still being written, the lives that are still being lived and the pain that still exists. This is just a reality check of a life that was changed in a blink of an eye. An angel that was taken too soon and his legacy that must continue on through his children.

People ask us, "How are you doing?" with that sad, head-tilted-to-the-side, and somber look of pain and anguish.

"We are good," I respond, with the same tilt, and somber smile that holds a lot of pain. "The kids are fine, getting big. Hasani is in his first year of high school now; Hannah is in the fifth grade and enjoys doing flips and is a social butterfly. And the baby, Haven, who is almost three years old. Wow, time sure does move quickly."

They usually continue on and I go about my life. This new, rebuilt life minus you, my beloved husband.

You were a great man, with a contagious smile that lit up the room as soon as you walked in. Everyone loved you. You were a man who truly came into his own, a wonderful, creative, funny man who loved his family. You were a great provider and as sweet as sweet potato pie that you enjoyed eating at Thanksgiving. I can't sing the praises of you enough. Not enough words in the English dictionary to describe you and do you justice, so I will stop here.

So with three children now and living in New York City, there is always something going on. Needless to say, my life is always moving and shaking. The kids keep me extremely busy and their schedules are crazy. They have auditions, basketball, dance, tutoring, music class and education, which is still so high on our list of priorities. Studying and homework becomes a huge part of our day.

You never know where your help will come from. We take it as it comes. I've learned to not question things—why and where "help" comes from. Just take it. We have learned to be very independent and do things on our own, so to accept help can be difficult at times.

Mom is your biggest cheerleader. She always wears her PAPD T-shirts, and with the same tilted head and somber look explains to EVERYONE how she lost her son on 9/11. She tells her friends in Maryland, "You know, I gotta go to New York 'cause of 9/11."

She almost brags about it. Not in a gloating way but because she really misses you. I try not to let everyone know. She does the opposite. I believe this is her way of dealing with her grief as well. She is so strong.

The children keep me young, and they remind me every day of you. You live on through them. Hasani's disposition and mannerisms are all you. Hannah looks like you but is very feminine and girly. They both are kind and compassionate children. I can't wait to see who they become as they grow up. I know you are looking down on them and smiling. You would be so proud.

Love always and forever,
Sonya

LETTER 07
YOU COULD FRY AN EGG ON THE
PAVEMENT

Noël Coward to Violet Coward
September 1921

By the time of his death in 1973, master playwright
Noël Coward had visited New York City more times
than he could recall. Indeed, during his prime, as he
flew back and forth between the theatres of London's
West End and Broadway that frequently staged his
work, he thought of it as his second home. This letter
was written to his mother at the beginning of that
period, in 1921, during his first trip to Manhattan.
Coward was twenty-one years old and had very little
money to speak of. What he did have, however, were
some manuscripts to sell and an endless supply of
enthusiasm. He was immediately smitten with
Broadway, and with Lynn Fontanne and Alfred Lunt,
two actors he mentioned to 'Snig'. Twelve years after
this letter was sent, as promised, Coward's new play
Design for Living, *starring Coward, Fontanne and Lunt,*
opened on Broadway.

THE LETTER

Brevort Hotel
New York
September, 1921

Darling old Snig,

In case you're wondering where your wandering boy is wandering, the answer is—anywhere and everywhere!

Why did nobody tell me that the streets of New York are so hot in the summer that you could fry an egg on the pavement (sorry, sidewalk!)—always supposing you had an egg!

Everybody who is anybody—and *everybody* wants to think they're *somebody*—goes out of town and they're now beginning to trickle back in with their Long Island tans. Even so I've met some fascinating folk.

Do you remember Lynn Fontanne? She played some small parts in London, was "adopted" by Laurette Taylor—now there's a character (and I've met her, *too*)—and came to New York. Well, she's had a huge success in a play called *Dulcy* (she's Dulcy). I went to see her opening night with her

fiancé, an actor called Alfred Lunt and, my dear,
a star was born. Well, two stars, actually, as
Alfred is also making a name for himself in these
parts.

They're quite wonderful and couldn't have been
kinder to me. They haven't any money either—
though they soon will have, I'm sure—and they
helped me keep body and soul together by sharing
their last crust (not quite that, really!). They're
going to be huge stars and, since we all know that
yours truly is going to be one too, we've decided
that, when that great day arrives, we shall act
together in a play I shall write for us and the
cosmos will have a new galaxy.

Really, darling, the theatre here is something to
wonder at. As a successful London playwright
myself—ahem! (Well, five weeks isn't a bad start!)
But I can tell you this is something in a different
world. The *speed*! Everybody seems to say their lines
at such a rate you'd think you wouldn't understand
a word—but you do! And then it suddenly struck
me—that's the way people actually *talk*. Wait till I
get back to Shaftesbury Avenue!!

Well, old Snig, that's all for now. Must rush or
the Astors and Vanderbilts will think I'm not
coming. Won't be long now till your dear son is
back to give you lots of hugs and bore everyone

with his stories and exploits, some of which actually *happened*!

Love, love, love.

LETTER 08
FIVE ACCIDENTS IN TWO MINUTES

Fred Allen to the State of New York
Insurance Dept
18 June 1932

*It was during the Golden Age of Radio in the 1930s
that American comedian and radio host Fred Allen
became a household name. His success on the airwaves
is undisputed: at the peak of its gag-filled, seventeen-
year run,* The Fred Allen Show *boasted upwards of
thirty million listeners. But it wasn't until a decade
after his death, upon publication of a collection of his
greatest letters, that the public learned of Allen's devo-
tion to this altogether more private form of
communication, one which allowed him to practise his
comedy in front of an audience of one. Arguably his
most amusing letter was a complaint, written in 1932,
most probably never sent, and addressed to the State
of New York Insurance Department.*

THE LETTER

June 18, 1932

State of New York Insurance Department
Office of the Special Deputy Superintendent
Liquidation of the Southern Surety
Company of New York
111 John Street, New York City.

Dear Sir:

The soullessness of corporations is something to
stun you. I am myself a victim; and instead of
being a man of wealth and honor to the community, I am now a relic of humanity just from the
hands of a surgeon who made an honest effort to
restore me to the form in which I grew while
reaching manhood's estate.

Let me review my case. I carry an accident
insurance policy in the New York Indemnity
Company, by terms of which the company agreed
to pay me $25 a week during such time as I was
prevented from working because of an accident.

I went around last Sunday morning to a new
house that is being built for me. I climbed the stairs,
or rather the ladder that is where the stairs will be

when the house is finished, and on the top floor I
found a pile of bricks which were not needed there.
Feeling industrious, I decided to remove the bricks.
In the elevator shaft there was a rope and a pulley,
and on one end of the rope was a barrel. I pulled
the barrel up to the top, after walking down the
ladder, and then fastened the rope firmly at the
bottom of the shaft. Then I climbed the ladder again
and filled the barrel with bricks. Down the ladder I
climbed again, five floors, mind you, and untied the
rope to let the barrel down. The barrel was heavier
than I was and before I had time to study over the
proposition, I was going up the shaft with my speed
increasing at every floor. I thought of letting go of
the rope, but before I had decided to do so I was so
high that it seemed more dangerous to let go than
hold on. So I held on.

Half way up the elevator shaft I met the barrel
of bricks coming down. The encounter was brief
and spirited. I got the worst of it but continued on
my way towards the roof—that is, most of me
went on, but much of my epidermis clung to the
barrel and returned to earth. Then I struck the roof
the same time the barrel struck the cellar. The
shock knocked the breath out of me and the
bottom out of the barrel. Then I was heavier than
the empty barrel, and I started down while the

barrel started up. We went and met in the middle of our journey, and the barrel uppercut me, pounded my solar plexus, barked my shins, bruised my body, and skinned my face. When we became untangled, I resumed my downward journey and the barrel went higher. I was soon at the bottom. I stopped so suddenly that I lost my presence of mind and let go of the rope. This released the barrel which was at the top of the elevator shaft and it fell five floors and landed squarely on top of me, and it landed hard too.

Now, here is where the heartlessness of the New York Indemnity Company comes in. I have sustained five accidents in two minutes. One on my way up the shaft, when I met the barrel of bricks, the second when I met the roof, the third when I was descending and I met the empty barrel, the fourth when I struck the barrel, and the fifth when the barrel struck me. But the insurance man said that it was one accident, not five, and instead of receiving payment for injuries at the rate of five times $25.00, I only get one $25 payment. I, therefore, enclose my policy and ask that you cancel the same as I made up my mind that henceforth I am not to be skinned by either barrel or/and any insurance company.

Yours sincerely and regretfully,

Fred Allen

LET ME TAKE YOU TO STRAWBERRY FIELDS
Yoko Ono to Various
19 August 1981

John Lennon famously wished he had been born in New York, and in 1971, not long after The Beatles had split, he began to make up for lost time by renting a two-room apartment on Bank Street in Greenwich Village with Yoko Ono. Less than two years later they moved to the Dakota building, where Lennon would spend the rest of his days. In 1981, a year after Lennon's death, Yoko Ono wrote an open letter which was published in various newspapers and sent to heads of state around the world. In it, she asked for donations of plants and rocks to be made to Strawberry Fields, a memorial to John Lennon in Central Park, opposite the Dakota. It remains there to this day and is visited by millions of people each year.

THE LETTER

In Memory of John Lennon, New York City has designated a beautiful triangular island in Central Park to be known as Strawberry Fields. It happens to be where John and I took our last walk together. John would have been very proud that this was given to him, an island named after his song, rather than a statue or a monument.

My initial thought was to acquire some English and Japanese plants and give them to the park commission to be planted in Strawberry Fields. But somehow that idea was not quite in the spirit of things. Then I remembered what John and I did when we first met over ten years ago. We planted an acorn in England as a symbol of our love. We then sent acorns to all heads of state around the world, inviting them to do the same. Many responded saying that they enjoyed the experience.

So, in the name of John and Yoko, and spirit of love and sharing, I would like to once again invite all countries of the world, this time to offer plants, rocks and/or stones of their nations for Strawberry Fields. The plants will eventually be forests, the rocks will be a resting place for traveling souls, the bricks will pave the lane John and I used to walk on and the circle where we used to sit and talk for hours. It will be nice to have the whole world in one place, one field, living and growing together in harmony. This will be the nicest tribute we could give to John. The acorn we planted a decade ago is now a tree. I would like to obtain a twig from it to be transplanted on the island. Maybe we could add a moonstone or a pebble from Mars, so as not to shut out the universe. The invitation is open!

Copies of this note will be sent to Mayor Koch, who has been a major inspiration behind the designation of Strawberry Fields, and to the heads of state throughout the world. Let me take you to Strawberry Fields.

Love,
Yoko Ono
August 19, 1981
New York City

'IT WILL BE NICE TO
HAVE THE WHOLE
WORLD IN ONE PLACE,
ONE FIELD, LIVING AND
GROWING TOGETHER IN
HARMONY'

— *Yoko Ono*

LETTER 10
THE LAST MAD EMPIRE ON EARTH
Dylan Thomas to Caitlin Thomas
25 February 1950

*On 23 February 1950, at the 92nd Street Young Men's
and Young Women's Hebrew Association on the corner
with Lexington Avenue (now more commonly known as
the '92nd Street Y'), Welsh poet Dylan Thomas took to
the stage and beguiled a thousand poetry aficionados
on the opening night of his first tour of America. Two
days later, dizzied by the reaction to his poetry and
overwhelmed by the urban jungle in which he found
himself, he wrote home to his wife, Caitlin. Thomas
toured the United States three more times over the
next few years, on each occasion beginning in New
York City. Sadly, it was on his fourth visit, in
November of 1953, at St Vincent's Hospital in
Greenwich Village, that Dylan Thomas died.*

THE LETTER

Midston House
22 East 38th Street
New York
Saturday Feb 25 '50

My darling far-away love, my precious Caitlin, my
wife dear . . .

Here, each night I have to take things to sleep: I
am staying right in the middle of Manhattan,
surrounded by skyscrapers infinitely taller &
stranger than one has ever known from the
pictures: I am staying in a room, an hotel room
for the promised flat did not come off, on the
30th floor: and the *noise* all day & night: without
some drug, I couldn't sleep at all. The hugest,
heaviest lorries, police-cars, firebrigades, ambu-
lances, all with their banshee sirens wailing &
screaming, seem never to stop; Manhattan is built
on rock, a lot of demolition work is going on to
take up yet another super Skyscraper, & so there is
almost continuous dynamite blasting. Aeroplanes
just skim the tips of the great glimmering
skyscrapers, some beautiful, some hellish. And I
have no idea what on earth I am doing here in the

very loud, mad middle of the last mad Empire on earth: – except to think of you, & love you, & to work for us. I have done two readings this week, to the Poetry Center of New York: each time there was an audience of about a thousand. I felt a very lonely, foreign midget orating up there, in a huge hall, before all those faces; but the readings went well . . .

I've been to a few parties, met lots of American poets, writers, critics, hangers-on, some very pleasant, all furiously polite & hospitable. But apart from on one occasion, I've stuck nearly all the time to American beer, which, though thin, I like a lot & is ice-cold. I arrived, by the way, on the coldest day New York had had for years & years: It was 4 above zero. You'd have loved it. I never thought anything could be so cold, my ears nearly fell off: the wind just whipped through that monstrous duffle. But, as soon as I got into a room, the steamed heat was worse: I think I can stand zero better than that, &, to the astonishment of natives, I keep all windows open to the top. I've been, too, to lots of famous places: up the top of the Empire State Building, the tallest there is, which terrified me so much, I had to come down at once; to Greenwich Village a feebler Soho but with stronger drinks; & this morning John Brinnin is driving us to Harlem . . .

And now it must look to you, my Cat, as though
I am enjoying myself here. I'm not. It's [a] night-
mare, night & day; there never was such a place; I
would never get used to the speed, the noise, the
utter indifference of the crowds, the frightening
politeness of the intellectuals, and, most of all,
these huge phallic towers, up & up & up, hundreds
of floors, into the impossible sky. I feel so terrified
of this place, I hardly dare to leave my hotelroom –
luxurious – until Brinnin or someone calls for me.
Everybody uses the telephone all the time: it is like
breathing: it is now nine o'clock in the morning, &
I've had six calls: all from people whose names I
did not catch to invite me to a little "poity" at an
address I had no idea of. And most of all most of
all most of all, though, God, there's no need to say
this to you who understand everything, I want to
be with you. If we could be here together,
everything would be allright. *Never* again would I
come here, or to any far place, without you; but
especially never to here. The rest of America may be
all right, & perhaps I can understand it, but that is
the last monument there is to the insane desire for
power that shoots its buildings up to the stars &
roars its engines louder & faster than they have ever
been roared before and makes everything cost the
earth & where the imminence of death is reflected

in every last power-stroke and grab of the great
money bosses, the big shots, the multis, one never
sees. This morning we go down to see the other
side beyond the skyscrapers: black Harlem, starving
Jewish East Side. A family of four in New York is
very very poor on £:14 a week. I'll buy some
nylons all the same next week, & some tinned stuff.
Anything else? . . .

Remember me. I love you. Write to me.

Your loving, loving Dylan

LETTER 11
THE BRIDGE – THE BRIDGE! GIVE US THE BRIDGE!

E. P. D. to the *Brooklyn Daily Eagle*
January 1867

Opened in 1883 and designed by a Prussian immigrant named John A. Roebling, the Brooklyn Bridge remains an awe-inspiring feat of engineering: a 1,595-foot suspension bridge spanning the East River, which in its heyday was the world's longest such structure. In 1867, sixteen years prior to its completion, and two years before construction began, this letter was sent to, and published in, the Brooklyn Daily Eagle*. It was written by a reader whose recent tour of Europe had convinced him of the need for such a bridge to connect New York City and Brooklyn. The letter also contains the first recorded reference to the 'Brooklyn Bridge', a name that was adopted for it forty-eight years later, in 1915.*

THE LETTER

To the Editor of the Brooklyn Eagle:

The project of communication with New York by
other means than our present Ferry System is one
upon which the writer has bestowed no little
reflection. A short time after returning from a
somewhat extended European tour, in connection
with a visit to the first World's Fair, of 1851, I
crossed the East River on the ice, and at that time
called to mind the various methods of river transit
I had witnessed in other countries. I had passed
over the Thames on London, Blackfriar's, and
Westminster bridges; and under it by the celebrated
Tunnel. However the latter method may suit the
easy-going Englishman, it will never find favor with
the enterprising inhabitants of Yankeeland; and
anyone will agree with me in this assertion, who
has had the curiosity to go down, down, and up,
up, those massive stone steps, and through that
gloomy excavation, which even the enlivening
strains of music which accompany the passage
cannot render cheerful.

But though England may be at fault in respect to
the matter of tunneling the Thames, there is one
enterprise which undoubtedly entitles her to great

48

credit. I refer to the noted bridge across the Menai Straits, extending from Carnavonshire to the Island of Anglesea, a distance, if I mistake not, of about 300 yards. This is acknowledged to be a work of great engineering skill and real utility; and in its construction Mr. Telford has amply verified the quaint saying of Sam Patch, that "some things can be done as well as others." The Menai Bridge is supported by vast stone pyramids formed into arches, from fifty to five hundred feet apart, beneath which flows the rapid whirling tide to and from the ocean. I do not now remember the width of this bridge, but recollect there were two carriage tracks and a footpath upon it, amply sufficient to accomodate the travel from Holyhead to London. The arches are semi-circular, on each side, adjacent to the main piers; the others are less segments, diminishing gradually as they approach the land; the crowns running parallel with the carriage-way admit a handsome entablature and cornice.

I crossed the Menai River in a small boat, passing beneath the arches, which gave a better idea of this magnificent structure—of its beauty, strength, and excellence, than could be obtained from above.

Often since then have I called to mind that splendid work of art, and almost as often ended my reflections with the pertinent inquiry: "Why may not a similar construction be made to unite New York and Brooklyn—the twin cities of American enterprise and Industry."

It is said Providence furnishes brains for the people according to the nature and structure of the country, and the wants and appreciation of its inhabitants. In America we have everything on a more magnificent scale than in the Old World. If then our rivers are wider, have we not a greater degree of enterprise and skill to be employed in erecting suitable structures across them? Let Europe boast of its towers, palaces, and cathedrals—works of by-gone ages and questionable utility—but let New York and Brooklyn join in the construction of a work of art and real usefulness, so that for centuries to come, "Brooklyn Bridge" will be spoken of in the same category with Westminster Abbey or St. Paul's of London, The Cathedral at Antwerp, St. Peter's of Rome, and other celebrities.

But I would combine more of the useful with the ornamental than any plan I have yet seen. "Will it pay?" is the first question with our people. I answer, "Make it pay." My plan is as follows:

Let a company be organized that shall purchase the land and water right from the junction of Main street with Fulton, in Brooklyn, to Chatham Square,

New York. Erect a continuous row of buildings—
stores beneath and dwellings above—rising higher
and higher till they reach the river. Let these be of
massive stone, between which and upon which the
bridge shall rest, with arches where streets shall
cross. The rising turrets can be used as chimneys to
carry the smoke into mid air, and the rent of these
dwellings will pay an excellent dividend. Arriving at
the water's edge, commence docking out and filling
up, until you have constructed a line of wharves and
piers one-fourth way across the river. On these erect
large storehouses, which shall also carry the bridge
as far as they go. The rest of these piers, wharves,
storehouses and granaries will be very great and pay
another excellent dividend. There can be stairs down
from the bridge through the storehouses to the
water, or various hoists to elevate goods and
merchandize to vehicles on the bridge. Also let there
be similar structures on the New York side, also
one-fourth way across the river toward Brooklyn.
Now, across the remaining half of the East River let
us have a firmly constructed suspension bridge—one
that will sustain two car tracks, two carriage ways
and two foot passages, or even more, if necessary.

Let there be large towers resting on massive
stone abutments, or rising from the bed of the
river, and above the bridge, and when connected

therewith, let each of these be formed into neat little shops or rooms, where travelers can stop and warm themselves in cold weather, and purchase the Morning *Herald*, *Sun*, *Tribune* and *Times*, or the Evening EAGLE; or get a cup of coffee or a cigar, or any other luxury. The rent of these shops would form another dividend! In fact, I think it would pay, to say nothing of the immense increase in the value of Brooklyn property.

I might, indeed, enlarge on this subject, and add a plan for making Brooklyn a port of entry, and constructing a Custom House and bonded warehouses in close proximity to the bridge. Then vessels from foreign ports could discharge their cargoes at our very doors, and Troy and Albany steamers or Jersey City ferries land their passengers in our very midst. By this I mean no disparagement to our sister city across the river. On the contrary, I would relieve it of a part of its almost intolerable burden. The streets are too crowded—space is too valuable there—and in the lower part of the city there is positively no room for expansion, and unless Brooklyn steps in and generously offers to relieve her, the merchants from the West, North and South will turn their attention to Boston and Philadelphia.

The bridge—the bridge! Give us the bridge!

E. P. D.

LETTER 12
THE FACTORY

Alfred Goldstein to Andy Warhol
15 November 1965

One can only imagine the parties that occurred on the fourth floor at 231 East 47th Street during the '60s, for this was Andy Warhol's Factory, the very studio in which his famous silkscreens were created on a daily basis. It was a veritable hotspot, welcoming a steady stream of visitors that included, amongst many, many others: Mick Jagger, Bob Dylan, Truman Capote, Allen Ginsberg, Salvador Dalí and William Burroughs. From 1965, the Factory even had a house band, of sorts, in the form of The Velvet Underground. No wonder the parties were so regular and legendary. With that in mind, it is hard not to sympathise with Warhol's landlord at the time.

THE LETTER

ELK REALTY, INC.
1107 BROADWAY
NEW YORK, N. Y. 10010
AREA CODE 212
WATKINS 4-3560

November 15, 1965

Mr. Andy Warhol
231 East 47 Street
New York, New York

Dear Mr. Warhol:

We have been advised that you have been giving
parties in the fourth floor space occupied by you.
We understand that they are generally large parties
and are held after usual office hours. We have
found that your guests have left debris and litter in
the public areas which you have never bothered to
clean. Further, we feel that a congregation of the
number of people such as you have had may be
contrary to various applicable governmental rules
and regulations and also might present a serious
problem with the Fire Department regulations.

Your lease, of course, does not permit such use and occupancy and you [are] hereby directed not to have any such parties in this building.

Very truly yours,

ELK REALTY, INC., Agents

(Signed)

Alfred R. Goldstein

President

ARG:sd

LETTER 13
LIBERTY, WE CHINESE DO LOVE AND
ADORE THEE

Saum Song Bo to Various

28 June 1885

Originally proposed by French activist Édouard René de Laboulaye and designed by sculptor Frédéric-Auguste Bartholdi, the Statue of Liberty was gifted to the United States by the people of France. It finally reached New York Harbor in June of 1885, a decade after the project was announced, but it would be another eleven months until the statue could be erected. The pedestal on which it was to stand was being built by the US and, with financing proving difficult, the American public had been asked to contribute to the fund both by the American Committee of the Statue of Liberty and Joseph Pulitzer, editor of the New York World. **This letter was written to, and published in, the** New York Sun **in response. Saum Song Bo, a citizen, penned the missive, outraged by the hypocrisy of such a request a mere three years after Congress passed the Chinese Exclusion Act – legislation which barred Chinese labourers from entering the country.**

THE LETTER

Sir:

A paper was presented to me yesterday for inspection, and I found it to be specially drawn up for subscription among my countrymen toward the Pedestal fund of the Bartholdi Statue of Liberty. Seeing that the heading is an appeal to American citizens, to their love of country and liberty, I feel that my countrymen and myself are honored in being thus appealed to as citizens in the cause of liberty. But the word liberty makes me think of the fact that this country is the land of liberty for men of all nations except the Chinese. I consider it as an insult to us Chinese to call on us to contribute toward building in this land a pedestal for a statue of liberty. That statue represents Liberty holding a torch which lights the passage of those of all nations who come into this country. But are the Chinese allowed to come? As for the Chinese who are here, are they allowed to enjoy liberty as men of all other nationalities enjoy it? Are they allowed to go about everywhere free from the insults, abuse, assaults, wrongs, and injuries from which men of other nationalities are free?

If there be a Chinaman who came to this country when a lad, who has passed through an

American institution of learning of the highest grade, who has so fallen in love with American manners and ideas that he desires to make his home in this land, and who, seeing that his countrymen demand one of their own number to be their legal adviser, representative, advocate and protector, desires to study law, can he be a lawyer? By the law of this nation he, being a Chinaman, cannot become a citizen, and consequently cannot be a lawyer.

And this statue of Liberty is a gift to a people from another people who do not love or value liberty for the Chinese. Are not the Annamese and Tonquinese Chinese, to whom liberty is as dear as to the French? What right have the French to deprive them of their liberty?

Whether this statute against the Chinese or the statue to Liberty will be the more lasting monument to tell future ages of the liberty and greatness of this country, will be known only to future generations.

Liberty, we Chinese do love and adore thee; but let not those who deny thee to us make of thee a graven image and invite us to bow down to it.

NEW YORK, June 28

SAUM SONG BO

LETTER 14
I'M SICK THINKING OF THE WHOLE MESS
Ralph Ellison to Ida Millsap
30 August 1937

In 1913, acclaimed novelist Ralph Ellison was born in Oklahoma City to Ida Millsap and Lewis Ellison, the latter of whom sadly died when Ellison was just three. In 1936, despite not having completed his music studies at Tuskegee University in Alabama and fully intending to return, Ellison headed for New York City to find work. He didn't make it back to Alabama. Instead, he was befriended by heavyweights from the Harlem Renaissance such as Alain Locke, Richard Wright and Langston Hughes. He also began to write fiction, including his opus Invisible Man, *in which the African American narrator moves to New York from the Deep South to find Harlem on the verge of unrest. It was in 1937, a year after reaching Harlem, that Ellison wrote home to his dear mother and described the injustice and poverty on his doorstep.*

THE LETTER

Dear Mama,

I haven't written because there really hasn't been anything new to write about. I am still living with Lang's aunt, but since her fall season has started I fear I'll have to find another place to stay. She is a very busy dressmaker, and people come in at all hours making my presence somewhat an inconvenience. They thought I would have had the job on the boat long before now, so I can't impose on them much longer.

I am very disgusted with things as they are and the whole system in which we live. This system which offers a poor person practically nothing but work for a low wage from birth to death; and thousands of us are hungry half of our lives. I find myself wishing that the whole thing would explode so the world could start again from scratch. Now one must have an education in order to get most any job, yet they don't give us opportunities to go to school. Look at your own life. You've lived these years since Dad died toiling from morning to night . . .

You've seen Herbert and myself grow up, and neither of us has a job. All those years and all that work, and not even a job to bring a dollar a week.

The people in Spain are fighting right now because of just this kind of thing, the people of Russia got tired of seeing the rich have everything and the poor nothing and now they are building a new system. I wish we could live there . . . You should see New York with its million of unemployed, the people who sleep in the parks and in doorways. The rich old women strolling down Fifth Avenue carrying their dogs which are better cared for than most human beings. Big cars and money to burn and right now I couldn't buy a hot dog. I'm sick thinking of the whole mess and I hope something happens to change it all . . .

The kids are now flying kites but they haven't started playing marbles. Those who can afford them are still wearing summer clothing and there is some talk and much talk of hope of buying new overcoats. Over the tops of flats and buildings you can see the kites sailing, and dipping, and rising like gulls riding the wind over a blue gulf, and you can hear the cries of the boys floating down, floating down to the street, like when you were around Look Out Mountain and you heard people climbing above you. On the streets are picket lines of people fighting for higher wages and shorter hours, and when you walk down some of the streets you wonder how some of the people are able to eat. If you walk down Eighth Avenue you can see the curb markets and fruit stores and seafood joints and if you come by around mealtime when the poor people are eating you can smell the fish frying and the hog maws and home fries. On the stands you see plenty of tropical fruit: mangoes, guavas and plantains, melons and yams. And on the corners you can buy bananas and fresh fish from vendors of pushcarts. All the fruit and fruit smells and fruit colors become all mixed with smells of washed and unwashed bodies and perfume and hair grease and liquor and the bright and drab colors of dresses and overalls, and that which the dogs leave on the sidewalk. I like to walk on such streets. Life on them is right out in the open and they make no pretence of being what they are not. The whore, the pimp, the ditch digger, the likker head, and the down-and-outer are all here trying to get along. It makes me very angry to think of the causes behind all the misery in the world, and the way it's all concentrated here in Harlem. I hope something happens to change it all.

Please let me hear from you soon, and you must remember not to worry about me. Tell me how your hip is doing and if you are able to walk.

Tonight's the night of the fight between Joe [Louis] and [Tommy] Farr. Already you can see the excitement rising and the police gathering. Just now a regiment of patrol passed all in blue and yellow trimmed uniforms and you can hear the horses' feet going cloppity clop, cloppity clop on the asphalt sounding all out of place amid the smacking whirr, smack, smack whirr of the rubber tires. Tonight there will be hundreds of cops in Harlem and much shouting of excited Negroes and most of the whites will stay out if Joe loses, and if he wins, they'll come up to see the fun. I'll write later. So until next time—

Love,
Ralph

THE BOWERY WAS ITS OWN WORLD
Martin Scorsese to Amanda Burden
13 March 2013

Originally a Native American footpath used by the Lenape tribe, the Bowery in Lower Manhattan is the city's oldest thoroughfare and a stretch of land that has brushed up against an eclectic assortment of neighbourhoods over the years. Its own fortunes have varied wildly over the years, transforming from a dirt trail to a theatre district to New York's skid row, and various other guises in between. So rich and varied is the area's history that in 2007 the Bowery Alliance of Neighbors formed in an effort to preserve its heritage, and in 2013 they launched the East Bowery Preservation Plan to fight against 'rampant over-development'. This letter, sent in support of the project to the City Planning Commission, came from Martin Scorsese.

THE LETTER

March 13, 2013

Amanda Burden, Chair
City Planning Commission
22 Reade Street
New York, NY 10007

Dear Chairwoman Burden,

I write to you today as a former resident of the
Bowery and a lifelong supporter of the protection
of its history, character and integrity.

Having grown up on Elizabeth Street, the neighborhood and residents of the Bowery became clear
catalysts for turning me into a storyteller. Whether
it's *Mean Streets* or *Gangs of New York*, the influence of
The Bowery — the grittiness, the ambience, the
vivid atmosphere — is apparent.

I urge you to insure that the Bowery remains
preserved and intact so its history continues to influence and inspire the upcoming artists of tomorrow.
The high-rise apartment buildings and condos only
create more chaos, more disruption and ultimately
offer The Bowery up to the elements of conformity.

For over 150 years, the Bowery was its own

world. With its own denizens, language, theater — in fact, its own genre of plays and vaudeville — it has become synonymous to other famous districts which helped make up what we know as the folklore of New York: Greenwich Village, Harlem, Broadway, etc.

I hope you will stand with me and my other supporters in acknowledging the East Bowery Preservation Plan. As I'm sure you are nostalgic to your hometown, I hope you sense my urgency in leaving the Bowery rich with history, artistry and distinction.

Sincerely,

Martin Scorsese

LETTER 16
THE SEAT OF THE EMPIRE
George Washington to the Mayor of New York
10 April 1785

On 25 November 1783, two months after the end of the Revolutionary War, history was made when the British Army finally vacated New York City: it was no longer a British colony. That same day, seven years after being forced from the area, General George Washington's Continental Army returned and paraded around the city, ending with a triumphant, public meal. Months later, Federalist lawyer James Duane became the 44th Mayor of New York City, and soon set about bestowing upon Washington the Freedom of the City. Washington responded with this letter, in which he calls New York 'the Seat of the Empire', widely believed to be the birth of New York State's nickname 'The Empire State'.

THE LETTER

To The Honble the Mayor, Recorder, Alderman &
Commonalty of the City of New York

Gentlemen, I receive your Address, and the freedom
of the City with which you have been pleased to
present me in a golden Box, with the sensibility
and gratitude which such distinguished honors
have a claim to. The flattering expression of both,
stamps value on the Acts; & call for stronger
language than I am master of, to convey my sense
of the obligation in adequate terms.

To have had the good fortune amidst the vicissi-
tudes of a long and arduous contest 'never to have
known a moment when I did not possess the
confidence and esteem of my Country.' And that my
conduct should have met the approbation, and
obtained the Affectionate regard of the State of
New York (where difficulties were numerous &
complicated) may be ascribed more to the effect of
divine wisdom, which had disposed the minds of
the people, harrassed on all sides, to make allow-
ances for the embarrassments of my situation,
whilst with fortitude & patience they sustained the
loss of their Capitol, and a valuable part of their

territory—and to the liberal sentiments, and great exertion of her virtuous Citizens, than to any merit of mine.

The reflection of these things now, after the many hours of anxious sollicitude which all of us have had, is as pleasing, as our embarrassments at the moments we encountered them, were distressing—and must console us for past sufferings & perplexities.

I pray that Heaven may bestow its choicest blessings on your City—That the devastations of War, in which you found it, may soon be without a trace—That a well regulated & beneficial Commerce may enrichen your Citizens. And that, your State (at present the Seat of the Empire) may set such examples of Wisdom & liberality, as shall have a tendency to strengthen & give permanency to the Union at home—and credit & respectability to it abroad. The accomplishment whereof is a remaining wish, & the primary object of all my desires.

George Washington

LETTER 17
THE TIME HAS COME TO PROTEST
W. E. B. Du Bois to Fifth Avenue Coach Co.
25 September 1946

*W. E. B. Du Bois was a writer, scholar, teacher, sociol-
ogist, historian and activist who worked tirelessly to
improve life for Black Americans. In 1895, he made
history as the first African American to earn a PhD at
Harvard; eight years later, his ground-breaking work
The Souls of Black Folk was published to wide acclaim,
and in 1909 he co-founded the National Association for
the Advancement of Colored People. Of his many
achievements, these are merely a few. Du Bois's
commitment to highlighting the many everyday injus-
tices dealt out to people of colour was unending, as
evidenced by this letter to the New York bus company
that was supposed to get him home. An apology of no
real length arrived days later, written by the bus
company's president, John E. McCarthy. It is unknown
whether the service improved.*

THE LETTER

New York City, September 25, 1946

Fifth Avenue Coach Co.

New York City

Gentlemen:

I write to complain of your service, especially the No. 2 route, which I use once or twice nearly every working day. There are usually too few buses on this route, far fewer than on any other main route. They often refuse to stop for passengers, even when not filled, and their conductors, and more especially their drivers (who do most of the talking to passengers), are insufferably rude. I stood this during the war, but it seems to me that the time has come to protest.

Tuesday, September 24, at about 5 p.m., I tried to board a No. 2 at Fifth Avenue and Fortieth Street. The first one swung out into the middle of the Avenue and refused to stop at my upraised arm, although it was plainly not filled. Its number marking as usual made it impossible to identify it. The next No. 2, plainly marked "168th St.," stopped and I got on and got a seat. Between 125th St. and 132nd Street, I heard the conductor say "155th St. only." But I thought I must have misheard. Before reaching 155th St., we were ordered off the bus. It was raining heavily; there is no car stop there; cabs were utterly out of sight and the street with three lines of traffic is dangerous to cross. I protested to the Conductor and demanded his number. He said 165; but he had no badge in sight and showed none, and I do not know whether or not he was telling the truth. Then the driver interrupted truculently and declared the car had been marked "155th St." which was not true when I boarded. There was nothing for me to do but to get out and walk in the pouring rain more than two long blocks uphill to my apartment at 409 Edgecombe Avenue.

I think this is an outrage; and when such treatment is added to the neglect of this route, the studied discourtesy of the employees, the failure to wear distinguishable badges, and the continued prayer of this company for added privileges in addition to the right to charge an exorbitant fare, I demand that something be done. The people of Harlem may be poor and black, but I trust this is not the reason for this treatment.

Very truly yours,

W. E. B. Du Bois

'I DEMAND THAT
SOMETHING BE DONE.
THE PEOPLE OF HARLEM
MAY BE POOR AND
BLACK, BUT I TRUST
THAT THIS IS NOT THE
REASON FOR THIS
TREATMENT.'
— *W. E. B. Du Bois*

LETTER 18
YOU ARE HER PEOPLE'S LAST HOPE
Jacqueline Kennedy Onassis to the Mayor of
New York
24 February 1975

By the time it opened to the public in 1913, New York's
Grand Central Terminal had been under construction
for a decade and amassed costs of more than $100
million. With forty-four platforms spread over
forty-nine acres, it is the world's largest train station,
and 750,000 passengers pass through its majestic
Main Concourse each day. Capacity aside, it is also
considered by many to be an architectural marvel, and
in 1967 was deemed to be a New York City Landmark.
Which is why, in 1975, when news broke of a plan to
build, atop this beloved station, a charmless skyscraper
designed by modernist architect Marcel Breuer, there
was pushback from all angles. One notable voice
belonged to former First Lady Jacqueline Kennedy
Onassis, who made her displeasure known first in a
letter to New York Mayor Abraham Beame, and later
at a press conference at the Terminal's much-loved
Oyster Bar.

THE LETTER

1040 FIFTH AVENUE
February 24, 1975

Dear Mayor Beame

I write to you about Grand Central Station, with the prayer that you will see fit to have the City of New York appeal Judge Saypol's decision.

Is it not cruel to let our city die by degrees, stripped of all her proud monuments, until there is nothing left of all her history and beauty to inspire our children? If they are not inspired by the past of our city, where will they find the strength to fight for her future?

Americans care about their past, but for short term gain they ignore it and tear down everything that matters.

Maybe, with our bicentennial approaching, this is the moment to take a stand, to reverse the tide, so that we won't all end up in a uniform world of steel and glass boxes.

Old buildings were made better than we will ever be able to afford to make them again. They can have new and useful lives, from the largest to the smallest. They can serve the community and bring people together.

Everyone, from every strata of our city, is wounded by what is happening—but feel powerless—hopeless that their petitions will have any effect.

I think of the time President Kennedy was faced with the destruction of Lafayette Square, opposite the White House. That historic 19th century square was about to be demolished to make way for a huge Eisenhower-approved Government Office Building. All contracts had been signed. At the last minute he cancelled them—and as he did so, he said, "This is the act I may be most remembered for."

Dear Mayor Beame—your life has been devoted to this city. Now you serve her in the highest capacity. You are her people's last hope—all their last hopes lie with you.

It would be so noble if you were to go down in history as the man who was brave enough to stem the tide, brave enough to stand up against the greed that would devour New York bit by bit. People now, and people not yet born will be grateful to you and honor your name.

With my admiration and respect

Jacqueline Kennedy Onassis

SO MUCH FOR THE POLICE SYSTEM

John DeGroot to the *Subterranean* newspaper
1847

*The New York City Police Department had been
running for just two years when, in 1847, this letter
appeared in the Subterranean, a local newspaper
founded in 1844 by a politician named Michael Walsh.
In it, a New Yorker named John DeGroot spoke of
witnessing an all-too-familiar instance of police
brutality against an African American citizen in Lower
Manhattan. The fate of all involved is unknown.*

THE LETTER

Mr. Editor:

I wish to state a few facts which occurred on
Saturday evening last in the Fifth Ward Station
House. I was passing through Church street about
half past 8 o'clock on the above evening, and
when near Duane Street, my attention was attracted
by a crowd of persons on the opposite side of the
way. I crossed over to learn the cause, when I saw
in the midst of them a colored man lying on his
back, struggling with half a dozen M. P.'s
[Municipal Police], and whenever the poor fellow
attempted to get upon his feet they would knock
him down with their Billies [batons], an instru-
ment loaded with lead. Feelings of humanity and
my duty as a citizen, prompted me [to] remon-
strate with the brute who struck him over the
head and arms. I told him it was not right so to
abuse the man, and asked him what crime he had
committed? His reply was, "*he's a d-d drunken nigger,
and we are going to take him to the Station House.*" I then
told them that unless they took him there in a
decent manner, I would complain to their captain.
If he is unable to walk, said I, get more men or
procure a cart and carry him. By this time the

78

poor fellow had got upon his feet; he said he had done nothing; told where he lived, and a friend offered to take him safely home, but he was refused. They then threw him on his back, and in that position dragged him to the Station House, a distance of over 500 yards. Humanity shudders at such acts. Had he been the worst of criminals, it could not have justified them in such brutality. I went to the Captain in behalf of the poor man, and stated to him how his men had acted; but before I had finished, the ignorant brutes laid hold of me (without the orders of the Captain) and thrust me in the street. I had scarcely landed upon the sidewalk, when two of them rushed out again, and carried me before their black-hearted Captain. His name is Tom Baker, well known in the Fifth Ward as a political sucker. There he was, surrounded by his brutal blackguards, and wishing to show off before them, delivered himself in the following style:

"Look a here, young man, you ought for to know better than for to go for to come here a complainin. My men knows their duty, and I knows mine, and we are all honest gentlemen; and ven ve vants adwice ve vill send for you. Now go away."

The poor negro, without any complaint being

made against him, was taken down below. So much for the *Police System*.

Yours, respectfully,

John DeGroot

LETTER 20
NEW YORK HAS SWALLOWED ME UP
Italo Calvino to Paolo Spriano
24 December 1959

Born in Cuba in 1923, Italian novelist and journalist Italo Calvino was one of the most important players in the world of postmodern literature thanks in no small part to his fantastical trilogy of folk tales Our Ancestors, *published throughout the 1950s. It was around the release of the series' final instalment, in 1959, that Calvino was chosen by the Ford Foundation, along with six other writers, to visit the United States on a literary tour. Calvino spent four of those months in New York City. Shortly before leaving for California he wrote a letter to his friend, the historian Paolo Spriano.*

THE LETTER

Hotel Grosvenor
35 Fifth Avenue
New York 3

New York, Christmas Eve 59

Dear Pillo,

I have not written to you yet, I never write to
anyone, New York has swallowed me up like a
carnivorous plant swallowing a fly, I have been
living a breathless life for fifty days now, here life
consists of a series of appointments made a week or
a fortnight in advance: lunch, cocktail party, dinner,
evening party, these make up the various stages of
the day which allow you constantly to meet new
people, to make arrangements for other lunches,
other dinners, other parties and so on ad infinitum.
America (or rather New York, which is something
quite separate) is not the land of the unforeseen,
but it is the land of the richness of life, of the full-
ness of every hour in the day, the country which
gives you the sense of carrying out a huge amount
of activity, even though in fact you achieve very
little, the country where solitude is impossible . . .

But really it is not this I mainly wanted to talk to you about, it's more to say that this country here knows nothing about us Europeans—and Russia here you can feel is part of Europe, and with no great differences either—because they are totally devoid of a sense of history. To put it briefly, I am beginning to understand something about America, but I have not got the time even to think never mind writing. I am leading the life of a businessman, because this is the real way to live in this city—I say business, but all I do is see publishers and have endless business lunches with them—I act as ambassador for an imaginary Italian Democratic Republic, because I feel it is my duty and responsibility to do so, being one of the few men of the left who has been given the chance to visit this country for six months. As a result, I have named myself ambassador and have delivered a lecture at Columbia University on recent Italian literature, where I squeezed in the Resistance, Gramsci, all the forbidden names about whom absolutely nothing is known here, and I will repeat this lecture around the universities: if nothing else it will serve to leave the official government representatives of culture with a bad taste in the mouth. I don't know anything about what is going on in the rest of Italy, I only have a subscription to *L'Eco della Stampa*. Here everyone's sole interest is Russia, nobody talks of anything else, the latest joke is: what is the difference between an optimist and a pessimist? The optimist is learning Russian, the pessimist Chinese. Now I am leaving New York, going to California. There I am going to hire a huge car. I have not driven yet. I am having a great time. I am following the party line, the party that is in the hearts of all of us. Say ciao to dear Carla. Happy New Year

Calvino

LETTER 21
THIS IS A VAST CITY

Pyotr Tchaikovsky to Vladimir Davydov
30 April 1891

On 17 April 1891, the great Russian composer Pyotr Tchaikovsky boarded the SS La Bretagne *in the French port of Le Havre and headed for the US to take part in a conducting tour of North America. He arrived in New York nine days later and began to prepare for his first task: conducting at the official opening of Carnegie Hall, then known as the Music Hall, on 5 May. In the week preceding the event, pleasantly surprised by the level of his fame in New York, Tchaikovsky wrote to his nephew Vladimir Davydov and described the scene.*

THE LETTER

April 30, 1891

Just received letters from Modia, Annette, and
Jurgenson. It is impossible to express how precious
letters are for one in my state. I was infinitely glad.
From day to day I keep a detailed diary and on my
return will give it to all of you to read—therefore,
I will not go into particulars. All in all, New York,
American customs, American hospitality, the very
sight of the city, and the unusual comforts of the
surroundings—all this is quite to my liking, and if
I were younger, I would probably derive great
pleasure from staying in this interesting, youthful
country. But I bear all this as if it were an easy
punishment, softened by favorable circumstances.
Thought and aspiration are one: homeward, homeward, homeward!!! There is some hope that I will
leave on the 12th. Everyone here pampers, honors,
and entertains me. It turns out that I am ten times
better known in America than in Europe. At first,
when they told me that, I thought that it was an
exaggerated compliment, but now I see that it is
the truth. Works of mine that are still unknown in
Moscow, are performed here several times a season,

and whole reviews and commentaries are written on them (e.g., *Hamlet*). I am far more a big shot here than in Russia. Is it not curious!! I was enthusiastically received by musicians at the rehearsal (till now there has been only one). But you will learn all the precise details from my diary. Now I'll say a few words about New York itself. This is a vast city, more strange and original than handsome. There are long one-storey houses, 11-storey buildings, and one building (a brand-new hotel) that is 17 storeys high. But in Chicago they went even further. There is a 21-storey building there!!! As for New York, this phenomenon can be simply explained. The city is situated on a narrow peninsula, surrounded by water on three sides, and can't grow any wider; therefore, it grows up. They say that in 10 years all the buildings will reach at least 10 floors. But for you the most interesting convention in New York is this: every little apartment, every hotel accommodation has a lavatory with a basin, bath, and washstand installed with hot and cold running water. Splashing in the bath in the morning I always think of you. Lighting is by electricity and gas. Candles are not used at all. In case of need, one acts differently than in Europe—namely, one rings and then says what is required through a tube, with one's mouth by the bell. Vice versa, if someone asks for me downstairs, they ring and then report through the tube who came or what they asked about. This is uncomfortable in view of my lack of English. No one except servants ever walks upstairs. The elevator runs constantly, going up and down at an incredible speed, to let the hotel's inhabitants and visitors in and out. As for the streets, but for the novelty that little houses alternate with huge buildings,—except for that peculiarity, the street itself is neither especially noisy nor especially crowded. The explanation is that there are hardly any cabbies or fiacres here. The traffic goes either by horsecars or on an actual railroad, with branches stretching over the whole vast city. Besides, in the morning, the entire population rushes to the East where "Downtown" is located, i.e., the part of the city with merchants' offices. In the evening all of them return home. They live as in London; every apartment is a separate house with several storeys, in a word, extending vertically, not laterally. That's enough for the time being. Soon I will write again to one of you. I embrace you, my dear one, also Modest and Kolia.

How soon, how soon?

Yours,

P. Tchaikovsky

'THIS IS A VAST CITY,
MORE STRANGE AND
ORIGINAL THAN
HANDSOME'
— Pyotr Tchaikovsky

LETTER 22
THE EMPIRE STATE BUILDING
Helen Keller to Dr John Finley

13 January 1932

Helen Keller was, by all accounts, an incredible woman. Born in Alabama in 1880, she is the author of twelve books, including an autobiography published when she was just twenty-two. A tireless activist and lecturer who campaigned for numerous causes, she was also deaf and blind as a result of a childhood illness. In 1932, after seeing a photograph of Keller atop the newly opened Empire State Building in Manhattan, Dr John Finley, President of the New York Association for the Blind, wrote to her and asked what she really 'saw' from that height. Keller responded with this magnificent letter – one of the most evocative descriptions of the skyscraper and its surroundings ever to have been written.

THE LETTER

January 13, 1932

Dear Dr. Finley:

After many days and many tribulations which are inseparable from existence here below, I sit down to the pleasure of writing to you and answering your delightful question, "What Did You Think 'of the Sight' When You Were on the Top of the Empire Building?"

Frankly, I was so entranced "seeing" that I did not think about the sight. If there was a subconscious thought of it, it was in the nature of gratitude to God for having given the blind seeing minds. As I now recall the view I had from the Empire Tower, I am convinced that, until we have looked into darkness, we cannot know what a divine thing vision is.

Perhaps I beheld a brighter prospect than my companions with two good eyes. Anyway, a blind friend gave me the best description I had of the Empire Building until I saw it myself.

Do I hear you reply, "I suppose to you it is a reasonable thesis that the universe is all a dream, and that the blind only are awake?" Yes — no doubt

I shall be left at the Last Day on the other bank
defending the incredible prodigies of the unseen
world, and, more incredible still, the strange grass
and skies the blind behold are greener grass and
bluer skies than ordinary eyes see. I will concede
that my guides saw a thousand things that escaped
me from the top of the Empire Building, but I am
not envious. For imagination creates distances and
horizons that reach to the end of the world. It is as
easy for the mind to think in stars as in cobble-
stones. Sightless Milton dreamed visions no one
else could see. Radiant with an inward light, he
sent forth rays by which mankind beholds the
realms of Paradise.

But what of the Empire Building? It was a
thrilling experience to be whizzed in a "lift" a
quarter of a mile heavenward, and to see New York
spread out like a marvellous tapestry beneath us.

There was the Hudson – more like the flash of a
sword-blade than a noble river. The little island of
Manhattan, set like a jewel in its nest of rainbow
waters, stared up into my face, and the solar system
circled about my head! Why, I thought, the sun and
the stars are suburbs of New York, and I never
knew it! I had a sort of wild desire to invest in a
bit of real estate on one of the planets. All sense of
depression and hard times vanished, I felt like

being frivolous with the stars. But that was only for a moment. I am too static to feel quite natural in a Star View cottage on the Milky Way, which must be something of a merry-go-round even on quiet days.

I was pleasantly surprised to find the Empire Building so poetical. From every one except my blind friend I had received an impression of sordid materialism — the piling up of one steel honeycomb upon another with no real purpose but to satisfy the American craving for the superlative in everything. A Frenchman has said, in his exalted moments the American fancies himself a demigod, nay, a god; for only gods never tire of the prodigious. The highest, the largest, the most costly is the breath of his vanity.

Well, I see in the Empire Building something else — passionate skill, arduous and fearless idealism. The tallest building is a victory of imagination. Instead of crouching close to earth like a beast, the spirit of man soars to higher regions, and from this new point of vantage he looks upon the impossible with fortified courage and dreams yet more magnificent enterprises.

What did I "see and hear" from the Empire Tower? As I stood there 'twixt earth and sky, I saw a romantic structure wrought by human brains and hands that is to the burning eye of the sun a rival luminary. I saw it stand erect and serene in the midst of storm and the tumult of elemental commotion. I heard the hammer of Thor ring when the shaft began to rise upward. I saw the unconquerable steel, the flash of testing flames, the sword-like rivets. I heard the steam drills in pandemonium. I saw countless skilled workers welding together that mighty symmetry. I looked upon the marvel of frail, yet indomitable hands that lifted the tower to its dominating height.

Let cynics and supersensitive souls say what they will about American materialism and machine civilization. Beneath the surface are poetry, mysticism and inspiration that the Empire Building somehow symbolizes. In that giant shaft I see a groping toward beauty and spiritual vision. I am one of those who see and yet believe.

I hope I have not wearied you with my "screed" about sight and seeing. The length of this letter is a sign of long, long thoughts that bring me happiness. I am, with every good wish for the New Year,

Sincerely yours,
Helen Keller

LETTER 23
NOTHING BUT GAS, GAS, GAS
Edna St. Vincent Millay to Cora and Norma Millay
22 September 1917

In the autumn of 1917, aged twenty-five, having recently graduated from Vassar College in Poughkeepsie, Pulitzer Prize-winning poet Edna St. Vincent Millay made the move to New York City's Greenwich Village. She remained there for eight years, at which point she and her husband left for Steepletop, their forever home in the town of Austerlitz in Columbia County. But this letter was written by Millay to her mother and sister back in 1917, soon after arriving in the Village. Millay was fresh-faced and eager to enjoy New York, but not, it seems, yet acclimatised to living in such a city.

THE LETTER

257 West 86th Street
Sunday, Sept. 22, '17

Dear Mother & Norma,
I have all the will in the world to write you a very
long letter—but the flesh is weak. I am in bed with
a curiously upset tummy. What *did* I eat?—If you
want to hear a nasty, unpleasant story, just listen
to the recital of what a perfect lady of your
acquaintance did last Friday night, vis. to wit, as
follows: . . .

Dinner, with Mitchell & Helen at the Plaza, and
after that the theatre & after that, T H I S !

We were standing on the corner of 5th Avenue
& 50th Street, waiting for a bus. We had walked
up from the theatre a way to get the air. But there
is no air on 5th Avenue, there is nothing but oil &
old gasoline & new gasoline—there is never one
breath of pure air—nothing but gas, gas, gas—but
people who live in New York walk there to get air.
Probably they do get it—all of it—& that's why it
blows to me so scummily. Well, this is what I did:
I had been feeling rarely funny all day, but didn't
know just what ailed me. But all of a sudden the

thought came to me, "*What* if I should have to up-swallow right here?" and I nearly died at the thought, but got a sort of control of myself & said to myself with shaky reassurance, "Ah, no, people don't do such things!" but then I thought, "Well, what if I *had* to?—then I guess I would!" and I felt very ill. Also I felt very weak & dizzy & queer & I began to lean on Helen & say, "I feel ill. I feel very ill. I am sorry," and I saw the machines going down the Avenue & up & smelled by the quart "That Good Gulf Gasoline" & saw Mitchell signal a taxi which did not see him but kept on going down the Avenue, & then there began to strike down into my mind the most beautiful streaks of colored light & I had the same wonderful dreams that I have when I take gas at the dentists (I *had taken gas!*) & I kept thinking "Oh, how beautiful! If I can only remember this to write it up!" & so I dreamed for what seemed quite a long while, and then, way, way off somewhere I heard two men speaking. One of them was saying, "There, that's right. Careful. Lift her up a little." And the other one said, "Yes, sir. Where to, sir?" or something like that. And I thought, "Wonder who's ill?—Poor girl. She must have fainted. Wonder who she is—why, it's I, that's who it is! It's my own self! That's what all

those colored lights & dreams meant,—I was
unconscious, I really fainted—oh, how wonderful—I'm so glad—now at last I know how it
feels!" because you see I had sort of flopped over
once or twice but I had always kept my head clear
& could hear & see; I had never lost conscious-
ness. This was very different, & it's comical to
consider how happy I was about it.—For one
thing, of course, I didn't feel ill any more, because
only my mind had become awake; I was quite
oblivious of my whole body. It was *so* beautiful &
comfortable! I had even forgotten for a few
blissful moments that I had a stomach.—But in a
little while I heard some funny little sounds, little
regular moans "Like mother used to make"
(forgive me, but I'm not very well yet,—and they
did sound so much the way mother sounded
when she used to feel faint!) And then I heard
Mitchell & Helen talking & realized that we were
in a taxi & that Mitchell was holding me in his
arms like an infant with my head back on his
shoulder. Next I remembered that I had a hand, a
left hand—& I thought I'd like to move it—but I
couldn't remember where it was. I thought I'd like
to open my eyes & look about for it, but I didn't
feel like opening my eyes. Then I became

conscious of a queer cold lump on my legs, ice-cold, & very heavy, & suddenly little horrid tingles began to rush through it & I knew it was my hand. And I thought "so *this* is the way it feels—cold, & dead & tingly—I'm glad I know— like when your foot's asleep, only colder, & more belonging-to-someone-else," and I made the most prodigious attempts—awful *pushes* with my mind, to lift that hand, & I might just as well have tried to lift Mitchell's hand just by thinking of it. But after many determined attempts it must be that it made some movement because Mitchell suddenly caught it in his & held it very hard & rubbed it & then it felt oh, so funny & after a while it was all right.

All this time, I hadn't thought of my tummy. But we stopped at a drug-store, & Helen got out & came back with some smelling-salts & they propped me up & I smelled & began to get back *all* my senses & the taxi went bumping & lurching on & oh, Lord! All at once I *knew*! & so did Mitchell, for he put his handkerchief into my hand, & said, "Stick your head out of the window, dear," & I did—& oh, Mother & Norma—it was Fifth Avenue, darlings, with thousands of people & millions of lights, but I didn't seem to care at

all, I was only happy that things had been decided
for me. Only I *did* try to avoid the policemen.—
And nobody knew me. There is a beautiful
anonymity about life in New York. And even
at the time I thought, "I'll bet people think
here's one young sport that's been on a beautiful
party!" And the joke was on them, because I
hadn't had a swallow,—excepting only a
very little very good beer—not half so much
as I had had with Rann every night at New
Hartford.

When I got out of the taxi at Helen's, tenderly
supported by Mitchell, who had been *such* a
darling, not seeming to mind at all, I looked
about on the wreckage I had wrought & turned to
the astonished cabby & said, "Oh, I'm *so* sorry!"
whereat he smiled in a most friendly kind way &
said, "Why, you can't help *that*, Miss!" & I got into
the house and proceeded to have a chill—I've
seen Nazimova do it when recovering from stage-
faint, & now I can do it every bit as well. So
Mitchell carried me upstairs & laid me on a bed &
went out to help the poor cabby, & Helen
undressed me & put me to bed—and *berlieve*
muh—I slept!

It's a ghastly loathsome tale, isn't it? But doesn't

it make a good story? I had to tell it all to
someone,—"& it might as well be you," poor
suffering family.

* * *

Goodbye, & please write,
Much love, Vincent.

IT IS BEYOND DESCRIPTION
Hart Crane to Grace Edna Hart and Elizabeth
Belden Hart
11 May 1924

*According to his published letters, it was early 1923
when modernist poet Hart Crane first began to plan
the work he became most known for:* The Bridge. *His
highly ambitious and much-lauded long poem was
inspired by the Brooklyn Bridge, a magnificent feat of
engineering that he could see from his home on
Columbia Heights. The poem took seven years to reach
print. In May of 1924, just over a year into the project,
Crane wrote to his mother and grandmother.*

THE LETTER

110 Columbia Heights
Brooklyn, New York
May 11th, '24

Dear Grace and Grandma:

I am told that this section of Brooklyn around here (Brooklyn Heights) is very much like London. Certainly it is very quiet and charming, with its many old houses and all a little different, and with occasional trees jutting up an early green through the pavements. I have just come back from breakfast and saw some tulips dotting the edge of one of the several beautiful garden patches that edge the embankment that leads down to the river. It certainly is refreshing to live in such a neighborhood, and even though I should not succeed in acquiring a room that actually commands the harbor view I think I shall always want to live in this section anyway. Mr. Opffer, who has such a back room in this house, has invited me to use his room whenever he is out, and the other evening the view from his window was one never to be forgotten. Everytime one looks at the harbor and the NY skyline across the river it is quite different, and the range of atmospheric effects is endless. But at twilight on a foggy evening, such as it was at this time, it is beyond description. Gradually the lights in the enormously tall buildings begin to flicker through the mist. There was a great cloud enveloping the top of the Woolworth tower, while below, in the river, were streaming reflections of myriad lights, continually being crossed by the twinkling mast and deck lights of little tugs scudding along, freight rafts, and occasional liners starting outward. Look far to your left toward Staten Island and there is the statue of Liberty, with that remarkable lamp of hers that makes her seen for miles. And up at the right Brooklyn Bridge, the most superb piece of construction in the modern world, I'm sure, with strings of light crossing it like glowing worms as the Ls and surface cars pass each other going and coming. It is particularly fine to feel the greatest city in the world from enough distance, as I do here, to see its larger proportions. When you are actually in it you are often too distracted to realize its better and more imposing aspects. Yes, this location is the best one on all counts for me. For the first time in many many weeks I am beginning to further elaborate my plans for my Bridge poem. Since the publication of my

"Faustus and Helen" poem I have had considerable satisfaction in the respect accorded me, not yet in print, but verbally from my confreres in writing, etc. Gorham has made the astounding assertion that that poem was the greatest poem written in America since Walt Whitman! Malcolm Cowley has invited me to contribute about a dozen poems to an anthology that he is planning to bring out through a regular publisher, and I am inclined to assent, as the other contributors are quite able writers and it will be some time before my *Bridge* poem is completed and I bring out my efforts in individual book form.

[...]

Much love, as always, your Hart

THEY WISH TO MAKE IT THEIR HOME
John V. Lindsay to Raymond F. Farrell
27 April 1972

In 1972, when this letter was written, John Lennon and Yoko Ono had been living in New York City for a year and were keen to make it their permanent home. They had also, much to the annoyance of the Administration, spent considerable amounts of time vocally opposing the Vietnam War and imploring their fans to vote against Nixon in the upcoming election. In retaliation, a deportation process was set in motion. This letter, written by the Mayor of New York in support of the couple's right to remain in the city, soon reached the White House. In 1975, the deportation order was overturned in court. A year later, Lennon was given a green card.

THE LETTER

THE CITY OF NEW YORK
OFFICE OF THE MAYOR
NEW YORK, N.Y. 10007

April 27, 1972

Hon. Raymond F. Farrell
Commissioner
Immigration and Naturalization Service
United States Department of Justice
119 D Street
N.E., Washington, D.C. 20536

Dear Commissioner Farrell:
I am writing this letter to you on behalf of John
Lennon and Yoko Ono who are currently facing
deportation proceedings initiated by your
Department.

I consider it to be very much in the public
interest, from the point of view of the citizens of
New York as well as the citizens of the Country, that
artists of their distinction be granted residence status.

They have personally told me of their love for
New York City and that they wish to make it their

home. They have made me familiar with the tragic hardship involved in their desperate effort to find Yoko's 8 year old child, Kyoko. I believe this is the type of hardship that our Immigration laws must recognize and the removal of the Lennons from this Country would be contrary both to the principles of our Country as well as the humanitarian practices which should be implemented by the Department of Immigration.

The only question which is raised against these people is that they do speak out with strong and critical voices on major issues of the day. If this is the motive underlying the unusual and harsh action taken by the Immigration and Naturalization Service, then it is an attempt to silence Constitutionally protected 1st Amendment rights of free speech and association and a denial of the civil liberties of these two people.

In light of their unique past and present contribution in the fields of music and the arts, and considering their talent to be so outstanding as to be ranked among the greatest of our time in these fields, a grave injustice is being perpetuated by the continuance of the deportation proceeding.

Very truly yours,

John V. Lindsay

MAYOR

LETTER 26
THE NEW YORK STATE LIFER
J.D. Salinger to the *New York Post*
December 1959

*Beyond the words contained in the slim selection of
novels and short stories he wrote and released into the
wild during his lifetime, it is difficult to know much of
J.D. Salinger, the man responsible for one of the most
influential books of the twentieth century, The Catcher
in the Rye. He very rarely made an appearance in
public, refused to give interviews on camera and
somehow succeeded in leaving no audio of his voice in
the public sphere. The last work of his to be published,
'Hapworth 16, 1924', appeared in print forty-five years
before his death. Which makes this letter, written in
1959 and sent to the New York Post by Salinger
himself, all the more noteworthy. It was printed in the
paper that December.*

THE LETTER

Several months ago, in an article in The Post entitled "Who Speaks for the Damned?" Peter J. McElroy cited that New York is one of the very few states that offers no hope whatever to the "lifers" in its prisons. In other words, once a man is sentenced to life imprisonment in New York State, there is no provision that after 20 or even 30 years he will go before a Board of Parole. The writer plainly thought the lack of such a provision cruel, even barbarous, and I surely agree with him, and so must a lot of other people. He went on to quote one of the New York State prison chaplains as saying, "Visitors' day at the prison is the most horrible of all for the lifers. They are almost completely forgotten." That rings horribly true. We can say, of course, that the lifer has brought his plight on himself. Or we can say, somewhat less virtuously, that justice has been done, and that's that. Justice, though, is at best one of those words that make us look away or turn up our coat collars, and justice-without-mercy must easily be the bleakest, coldest combination of words in the language. If no mercy may be legally shown to the New York State lifer, then at least some further legislation should be provided so that when a man in New York is sentenced to life imprisonment the real terms of his sentence are pronounced in full, for all the world to hear. Something on this order, perhaps: "You will be imprisoned in a New York State penal institution for the rest of your natural life. If, however, after 20 years or 30 years you not only are truly penitent but have shown, in the indifferent opinion of New York State, a very marked improvement in character—comparable in quality and depth to that of the average free citizen of New York—you will then be permitted, slowly, charitably, intelligently, at the taxpayers' expense, to rust to death in a sanitary, airy cell superior in every way to anything offered in the 16th century."

This is all a matter for action, though, not irony. Can it be brought to the attention of the Governor? Can he be approached? Can he be located? Surely it must concern him that the New York State lifer is one of the most crossed-off, man-forsaken men on earth.

J.D. SALINGER

LETTER 27
A PALE HUMANITY PATTERS ALONG
Rebecca West to Winifred Macleod
2 November 1923

British novelist and critic Rebecca West was born Cicily Fairfield in London in 1892, and was eight years old when her father, by all accounts a useless man, fled the family home, never to return, soon after which her mother relocated her family to Edinburgh. As a young lady, West became a staunch feminist and literary critic, and in 1912 began a relationship with H. G. Wells, whom she met after he took offence at her negative review of his new novel. In 1923, exhausted and emotionally fraught after splitting from Wells following what can only be described as a stormy relationship, West reluctantly made her way to the US to embark on a lecture tour – the first of many that she would go on to make. On 2 November, upon leaving New York for Philadelphia, she wrote to her sister Winifred and, without pulling so much as a punch, made known her opinion of New York and, more generally, the people of that great country.

THE LETTER

The Bellevue Stratford
Philadelphia
2 November 1923

Dear Podgers,

I haven't had a moment to write a line before. I had a fair voyage on the Mauretania—was only a little uncomfy the first day which was very rough, but then started an attack of colitis and had bad tummy pain till a day off New York. When the Immigration officer came aboard I went before him and got my passport visaed and so on. After I had done this a steward came up to me and said—"The Chief Immigration Officer wishes to see you." I nearly died—when I got down to him he said, "I have a letter from Mr Curran the Commissioner of Labor asking you to treat me with special courtesy and to give you this pass through the Customs." So that was all right. It turned out that Henry James Forman had written to Curran who is a friend of his.

The view going up New York Harbour is gorgeous. Miles and miles of shore covered with low dock buildings—incredibly strange erections of a Robot civilisation—then this cluster of skyscrapers white and slim like lilies. The Statue of Liberty is a washout—she gets her stays at the same place as Queen Mary. I was met by Miss Laurent—& my publisher's publicity agent—& my London literary agent Andrew Dakers who happened to be in N.Y. (most unfortunately as you will hear), and my lecture agent's manager. I then had a hectic day. Two hours with reporters—five of them, during which one or two of them tried to make me say something unwise. One published an impertinent interview—"when asked if she were a literary protégé of Mr Wells she quickly changed the subject." The rest were all right. I was then taken off to a literary tea at Somerset Maugham's—he has a small flat here just now while a play is being produced—not so nice as mine—The rent unfurnished is $5000 a year. Then I wound up with a dinner of the business people—Sunday I spent in the same way. I woke up at 9 with a start and found a pale sad looking woman in my room. She said, "I am Miss Something of the Something or Other," and opened a notebook, and leaned over the end of my bed. "We would like to know, Miss West," she said in an unutterably tired and flat voice, "if you would like to marry an American." One way and another I wasn't alone till eleven that

night. Among other people I saw a woman theatrical manager who wants to put on a dramatic
version of *The Return of the Soldier* in January. She has
paid various playwrights $3000 to prepare versions
of it and hasn't got anything that gets the essence
of the play. It was a fascinating couple of days—the
air in New York is intoxicating—the architectural
beauty sublime—but I simply cannot convey to you
how unlike America is to what it says it is and gets
other people to say it is. I have been in three places
now—New York, Springfield (Mass.)—and here—
everywhere the women are hideous and beyond all
belief slovenly. A certain number are good looking
between the ages of seventeen and twenty five—
they get even that good looks simply by force of
slimness and careful management—There are very
few good looking women of thirty—the middle
aged women are repulsive wrecks—bad skins, and
untidy though elaborately dressed hair—and at all
ages the most terribly bad carriage. They wear very
expensive and solid clothes which they huddle
round them in such a way as to spoil all their
lines—and they walk and dance with their feet
wide apart. Almost every woman not theatrical who
has spoken to me has worn an untidily adjusted
hairnet dragging over her forehead and round the
nape of her neck. Their utter and complete lack of

sex attraction is simply terrifying. Not that it
matters—for the men seem entirely lacking in
virility. They wear spectacles almost as commonly as
the Germans—and they are beyond belief slow. The
mechanical side of life here whirls—telephones,
taxis, trolleys—but a pale humanity patters along in
the midst of it. (The only attractive and thoroughly
male personality I met in New York was my
publisher George Doran—an elderly man—between
sixty and seventy—and he turned out to be a
Canadian.) They are slow in speech, slow in movement, slow in thought. The irritation of <listening>
(receiving) a telephone message from an American
is almost past belief—the service is incredibly quick
and good—one is connected at once—and then a
slow, dry voice drawls interminably.

* * *

The journey from Philadelphia here (I am finishing
this letter in Chicago) took eighteen hours—The
first six followed alongside the Susquehanna and
Julietta Rivers. Nothing in the world could convey
the wistful beauty of American river scenery—the
serenity of the wooded heights—wave-like in their
skyline—the beauty of the wide shallow waters. I
was adopted in the train by a charming old Texan,

who called me "Ma'am," paid me old fashioned
compliments ("If I may ask, Ma'am, how is it that
such a charming lady as yourself have escaped
matrimony?") insisted on treating me to all my
meals, and escorted me to my hotel here. The
amount of attention one gets from men here would
turn one's head if one didn't look round at the
sallow hags of American women and realise that
the standard is very different from Europe! This
hotel is an extraordinary palace in the Italian style
built on the edge of Lake Michigan—today a grey
waste of thundering breakers. I really must stop
and put in some work on my next lecture. I won't
make much money out of this but it is gorgeous
fun—and if there is any trouble enough people in
New York feel friendly to give me a graceful exit.
Very much love.

Anne

LETTER 28
HERE WE ARE IN NEW YORK

Alexis de Tocqueville to Louise Madeleine Le
Peletier de Rosanbo

14 May 1831

*In 1831, French sociologist and political theorist Alexis
de Tocqueville was commissioned by the French government to travel to the United States – along with friend
and magistrate Gustave de Beaumont – with a view to
studying its prisons. For nine months they did exactly
that, writing and publishing a report on the country's
prison system upon their return. In 1835, however,
Tocqueville released the first volume of something arguably more valuable:* Democracy in America (De La
Démocratie en Amérique), *a highly influential book
containing his wider observations of American society
that drew plaudits in both France and the United
States. This letter to his mother was written in New
York, at the beginning of that long journey.*

THE LETTER

[...]

Here we are in New York. From a Frenchman's
perspective, it looks disarmingly weird. There isn't a
dome, a steeple or a large edifice in sight, which
leaves one with the impression that one has landed
in a suburb, not the city itself. At its very core,
where everything is built of brick, monotony rules.
The houses lack cornices, balustrades, carriage
entrances. Streets are ill paved, but pedestrians have
sidewalks.

Lodging was a problem at first because
foreigners abound at this time of year and because
we sought a pension, not an inn. At last we found
one that suits us perfectly, on the most fashionable
street in town, called Broadway. As luck would have
it, M. Palmer, the Englishman I mentioned earlier,
had already found accommodations in this
boarding house. Our shipboard friendship and
especially the interest he is taking in our mission
have led him to oblige us whenever and however
possible. Best of all are the amenities offered by

Americans. They beggar description. Men of every class seem to compete for the honor of being most cordial and useful. The newspapers, which report everything, announced our arrival and expressed the hope that people would come forward to assist us. They have outdone themselves. All doors are open and welcoming hands extended at every turn. I, for whom diligences and inns have always been the tiresome appanage of travel, find these new conditions most agreeable.

One difficulty that has hampered us ever since we left France, and which we have begun to overcome, is language. In Paris, we fancied we knew English, not unlike collegiate school graduates who think that their baccalaureate is a certificate of learning. We were soon disabused of that notion. All we had was a basic vehicle for making rapid progress. We truly drove ourselves during the ocean crossing; I remember days on a windswept deck translating English when it was difficult to hold a pen. Unfortunately, with so many French speakers aboard we could always fall back on our native language. Here the situation is different. As no one speaks French, we have had to give it up. Our conversation is entirely in English. It may sound pitiful, but at least we make ourselves understood and understand everything. Interlocutors even tell

us that we show great promise. If we do end up
mastering the language, it will be an excellent
acquisition. The benefits we've already reaped illus-
trate for me the foolishness of a Monsieur de
Belisle, who travels to lands where he cannot
converse. One might as well take strolls in one's
room with the windows shuttered.

No doubt you would like to know, my dear
Mama, how we spend our days. We rise between 5
and 6 and work until 8. At 8 o'clock the breakfast
bell rings. Everyone convenes punctually. Afterward
we visit several establishments to interview men
with knowledge of matters that concern us. We
return for dinner at 3 o'clock. Between 5 and 7 we
put our notes in order. At 7 we go out and
socialize over tea. This way of life is most agreeable,
and I believe eminently sane. But it flouts all our
assumptions. Thus, we were quite surprised at first
to see women appearing at the breakfast table with
faces carefully made up for the day. We are told that
this is customary in all private houses. Paying visits
to a lady at 9 in the morning is not thought
improper.

At first we found the absence of wine from
meals a serious deprivation, and we are still baffled
by the sheer quantity of food that people somehow
stuff down their gullets. Besides breakfast, dinner,

and tea, with which Americans eat ham, they have very copious suppers and often a snack. So far, this is the only respect in which I do not challenge their superiority; they, on the other hand, reckon themselves superior in many ways. People here seem to reek of national pride. It seeps through their politeness.

'FROM A FRENCHMAN'S PERSPECTIVE, IT LOOKS DISARMINGLY WEIRD . . . [BUT] ALL DOORS ARE OPEN AND WELCOMING HANDS EXTENDED AT EVERY TURN'

— *Alexis de Tocqueville*

DEAR NEW YORK CITY
Spalding Gray to New York City
12 September 2001

Born in Rhode Island in 1941, Spalding Gray arrived in New York aged twenty-six, beginning a love affair that would last the rest of his life. Throughout those years in the city, he immersed himself fully in the alternative theatre scene. His first monologue, 'Sex and Death to the Age 14', came in 1979. Many others followed, as did awards, movie roles, a family and, sadly, mental health problems which, coupled with injuries sustained in a car accident in 2001, led to him taking his own life in 2004. He wrote this letter to New York City the day after the World Trade Center towers were brought crashing to the ground.

THE LETTER

12 September 2001

Dear New York City,

For 34 years I lived with you and came to love you. I came to you because I loved theater and found theater everywhere I looked. I fled New England and came to Manhattan, that island off the coast of America, where human nature was king and everyone exuded character and had big attitude. You gave me a sense of humor because you are so absurd.

When we were kids, my mom hung a poster over our bed. It had a picture of a bumblebee, and under the picture the caption read:

"According to all aerodynamic laws, the bumblebee cannot fly because its body weight is not in the right proportion to its wingspan. But ignoring these laws, the bee flies anyway."

That is still New York City for me.

PERMISSION CREDITS

LETTER 1 Anaïs Nin, letter 'I'm in love with NY' to Henry Miller, December 3, 1934, published in *A Literate Passion: Letters of Anaïs Nin & Henry Miller: 1932–1953*, Harcourt Brace Jovanovich, 1987, copyright © 1987 by Rupert Pole, as Trustee under the Last Will and Testament of Anais Nin; and the Anaïs Nin Trust. Reprinted by permission of Houghton Mifflin Harcourt Publishing Company and the Anaïs Nin Trust. All rights reserved.

LETTER 3 Edmund White, letter 'We Shall Overcome' to Ann and Alfred Corn, June 1969, published in *The Violet Quill Reader* ed Bergman, and *Letters of the Century: America, 1900-1999* ed Lisa Grunwald, Stephen J. Adler, copyright © 2009 by Edmund White. Reproduced by permission of the Clegg Agency.

LETTER 4 Kahlil Gibran, letter "Shadows run after me" May 1, 1911, published in *Beloved Prophet: The Love Letters of Kahlil Gibran and Mary Haskell, and Her Private Journal*, 1972, Penguin Random House USA Inc.

LETTER 5 E.B. White, letter 'They are being had' to Harold Ross, January 1950, published in *The Letters of E.B. White Revised Edition*, HarperCollins 2006, pp.292-293. Reproduced by permission of ICM Partners.

LETTER 6 Sonya Houston, letter 'You would be so proud' to Uhuru Gonja Houston, 2011, published in *The Legacy Letters: Messages of Life and Hope from 9/11 Family Members*, Penguin Random House, 2011, pp.13-15. Reproduced with kind permission from Tuesday's Children.

LETTER 7 Noël Coward, letter 'You could fry an egg on the pavement' to Edna Ferber, September 1921, published in *The Letters of Noël Coward*, Bloomsbury, ed, Barry Day, 2014, copyright © NC Aventales AG 1921. Reproduced by permission of Alan Brodie Representation Ltd, www.alanbrodie.com

LETTER 9 Yoko Ono, open letter 'Let me take you to Strawberry Fields', 19 August 1981, https://daytrippin.com/2017/12/04/the-story-behind-john-lennons-strawberry-fields-in-new-york/, copyright © Yoko Ono Lennon, 2020.

LETTER 26 J.D. Salinger, letter 'The New York State lifer', December 9, 1959, *New York Post*. Reproduced by permission of the Estate of the author.

LETTER 27 Rebecca West, letter 'A pale humanity patters along' to Winifred Macleod, November 2, 1923 from *Selected Letters of Rebecca West*, Yale University Press, 2000. Reproduced by permission of Peters Fraser & Dunlop (www.petersfraserdunlop.com) on behalf of the Estate of Rebecca West.

LETTER 29 Spalding Gray, letter 'Dear New York City' published in *Life Interrupted: The Unfinished Monologue*, 2005 by the Estate of Spalding Gray. Used by permission of Crown Books, an imprint of Random House, a division of Penguin Random House LLC; and WME. All rights reserved.

ACKNOWLEDGEMENTS

It requires a dedicated team of incredibly patient people to bring the Letters of Note books to life, and this page serves as a heartfelt thank you to every single one of them, beginning with my wife, Karina — not just for kickstarting my obsession with letters all those years ago, but for working with me as Permissions Editor, a vital and complex role. Special mention, also, to my excellent editor at Canongate Books, Hannah Knowles, who has somehow managed to stay focused despite the problems I have continued to throw her way.

Equally sincere thanks to all of the following: the one and only Jamie Byng, whose vision and enthusiasm for this series has proven invaluable; all at Canongate Books, including but not limited to Rafi Romaya, Kate Gibb, Vicki Rutherford and Leila Cruickshank; my dear family at Letters Live: Jamie, Adam Ackland, Benedict Cumberbatch, Aimie Sullivan, Amelia Richards and Nick Allott; my agent, Caroline Michel, and everyone else at Peters, Fraser & Dunlop; the many illustrators who have worked on the beautiful covers in this series; the talented performers who have lent their stunning voices not just to Letters Live, but also to the Letters of Note audiobooks; Patti Pirooz; every single archivist and librarian in the world; everyone at Unbound; the team at the Wylie Agency for their assistance and understanding; my foreign publishers for their continued support; and, crucially, my family, for putting up with me during this process.

Finally, and most importantly, thank you to all of the letter writers whose words feature in these books.

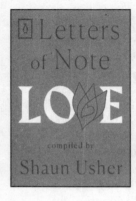 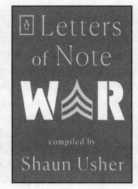